DAY SIX

A critical analysis of:

Evolution

Creation

Religion

Catholic Church

By Joe Allard

Copyright © 1991
by Joe Allard

Published by
Joe Allard Enterprises
74490 Laurelwood Road
Rainier, OR 97048

Day Six

Production by *Frontier Publishing*, Seaside, OR

All rights reserved. No part of this book may be commercially reproduced in any form or by any means without permission in writing from the author's designated representative.

Printed in the U.S.A.

Table of Contents

Chapter   **Page**

PART I: EVOLUTION

1 The Earth—How Did It Came Into Existence?......3
    The Existing Earth 3
    Space 7
    Time 7
    Light 8
2 Theories of Evolutionists......................................12
3 Strata—Is it a Reliable Source of Information? .15
4 Mars and Strata 21
    Strata On the Surface of the Earth 26
5 Piltdown Man..32
    Man..33
6 Fossils 41
7 Living Fossils 43

PART II: CREATION

8 Is There a God?..53
    The Hebrew Bible 53
    Many Religions 55
    Is There a God? 56
    Time and Space 57
9 The Personification of Wisdom 60
10 Day Six..67

Table of Contents

Chapter   **Page**

PART III: RELIGION

11 History of Man and Signs Given Him 73
12 Misinterpretation of the Dove and the Rock 85
13 Jesus, The Way 93
      The Precedent Case 95
14 Lucifer and the Curse 111
      Lucifer 111
      Peter Unlocks the Plan to Salvation 117

PART IV: CATHOLIC CHURCH

15 Pagan Mass 123
      Rome 123
      Different Religious Beliefs 133
16 Catholic Cross 146
      The Evolution of the Cross 151
      The End of the Roman Empire 153
17 Catholic 156
18 The Cross and the Inquisition 170
      Easter 180
      Christmas 181
19 Making the Final Decision 187
      First Day 187
      Second Day 188
      Third Day 189
      Fourth Day 191
      Fifth Day 194
      Sixth Day 195

Order Form .... Back Page

Preface

In 1930 Joe Allard followed years of Bible study by beginning a compilation of information to present his comprehension of what he had learned, and was still learning, about creation, evolution, and how and why various religions developed.

Eleven years ago, when Mr. Allard was 80 years old, he bought his first computer and began the task his more than 50 years of accumulating facts and information had prepared him for — writing the manuscript for this book.

In spite of a crippling stroke that limited his typing ability to the use of one finger, he laboriously continued placing his thoughts into manuscript form. Such was his commitment that three-fourths of the material for this book was typed under that handicap.

Not only has extensive historical and biblical study gone into this project, but Mr. Allard's observations during a varied and successful business career have aided in preparing him for presenting this publication. For 18 of 22 years in the dental support profession he owned and operated his own dental laboratory in Los Angeles. Following his retirement in 1942 he purchased and managed property in California, including operation of his date and avacado farms. In 1962 he moved to Rainier, Oregon.

Part I

Evolution

Chapter 1

The Earth — How Did It Come Into Existence?

THE EXISTING EARTH

Those who believe in a Supreme Being (*called God*) say that God created the Earth. Those who do not believe there is a God say that it all started from a so-called "**Big Bang.**" The big question is how was it done? Did some mysterious, invisible God create the Earth? Or, did things come into existence by the Big Bang?

This treatise will search for information, wherever we can find it, that will help us SOLVE this question That is, was this Earth created by a Supreme Being or did it come into existence by chance according to the theories of evolution?

Some parts of the world's history will be studied in a unique analytical method in order to understand its significance. And religion will be spread out for examination and investigation. The Catholic Church will be examined to see how it evolved from Roman paganism to this present day.

Evolution will be looked into to see if it is based on **scientific facts or on theory**. How "physical matter" came into existence. And a few other miscellaneous subjects will be studied in order to tie all these other subjects together so we can understand them and also for support of thought. **So don't be surprised** if a few other subjects are examined that do not pertain to the

Day Six

study of "How the Earth came into existence."

Those who believe that God created the Earth and all that is on it in **six days** are called fundamentalist. As stated in Webster's New World Dictionary fundamentalism is:.

> FUNDAMENTALISM ... 1. orthodox religious beliefs based on a ***literal* interpretation** of the Bible (e.g., *complete acceptance* of the story of creation as given in Genesis and rejection of the theory of evolution, and regarded as fundamental to the Christian faith.)

Every one has the inalienable right to believe what he or she wants to believe even if it cannot be proven or is ridiculous. Just read the material about some philosophers' interpretations of the Bible on how to get to the happy hunting grounds — if you can hold down this junk you have a cast-iron stomach. It is your privilege to believe any nonsense you care to believe.

This book was inspired to be written because of a Tennessee law that *forbid the teaching in public schools* of any theory that denied the Bible story of creation.

There was a teacher (John T. Scopes) in Dayton, Tennessee, who said he could not teach biology without explaining evolution because he was dealing with living tissues. ***Life* had to be accounted** for in some way. He expressed his belief that living things came by accident millions of years ago. The encyclopedia *Americana* gives this account of his trial.

> The so-called "evolution trial" of John T Scopes, youthful teacher of biology in the local high school, was held here in July 1925, **as a *test* case** to determine the valid-

The Earth — How Did It Come Into Existence?

ity of a Tennessee statue enacted in March of that year, under which it became unlawful for the public schools of the state to teach **any theory denying the Bible story of creation.** The defense enlisted the support of Clarence Darrow, Dudley Field Malone and Arthur Garfield Hays, while the prosecution was headed by William Jennings Bryan, an ardent supporter of the law. The verdict of **<u>GUILTY</u>** returned against the defendant was later set aside by the state supreme court on a technicality and thus no ruling was made upon the constitutionality of the measure.

Encyclopedia Americana (see Dayton, Tenn.)

The citizens of Dayton, Tennessee, framed-up this test trial to put the little town of Dayton on the map — and it sure did. But it became a ridiculous trial because neither side had a thorough knowledge of the subject.

Darrow, the evolutionist, claimed that the Earth must be millions of years old because the original crust was a snarled bed of melted rock — called gneiss — that was formed by intense heat and water. So, evolution is a **"*science*" that proves the Earth was not made in one day.** Bryan (a fundamentalist) insisted that God created the Earth in one day because the Bible said so. This trial soon became known as the "Monkey Trial" because Darrow claimed life originated from a rock, and, in time, man evolved from the monkey. Both attorneys made monkeys of themselves by not knowing the true facts.

The Tennessee State Supreme Court couldn't understand "who done it" so it was set aside on a technicality. This controversy is still being fought in different states. Though nothing *new has been discovered*, the monkeys are still at it!

Day Six

Almost everyone knows about the theory of evolution. Evolution scientists tell us how life started on this planet and the subsequent development of man. The thoughts concerning evolution today are varied: perhaps life came to this Earth on a comet; or maybe, some peculiar mixture of chemicals in the ocean came to life. Maybe somehow an atom of a rock decided to reproduce itself, and start living. Who knows how and when it all began? If the evolutionists do know; how did they find it out?

Scientists have discovered many marvelous laws of nature, such as gravity, the coming of an eclipse to the very second, and calculation of a comet's return. They have fallen into a trap by mixing *theory* with true science.

We will also investigate the theories of the theologians, who interpret the word of the Bible to suit their doctrine. Anything in the Bible that does not agree with the theologian's ideas on religion never seems to be found. The doctrine of the church is foremost. This is also true with the evolutionist who searches the world over for evidence to substantiate his theory but discards all evidence to the contrary.

Neither side is on the right path. They are false leaders because they do not go to the true source of knowledge, which is not found in man-made religion or a hole in the ground! So far the theologians are still enlarging their doctrine and the scientists are still digging holes in the Earth. *Knowledge* is drawn from undisputable facts that have been thoroughly investigated, checked and cross-checked.

The truth is very hard to find but it's there some place. If you had a bundle of money that was mixed with some counterfeit would you throw it all away? No. You would carefully discard the counterfeit, keeping that which is good. Let's do the same thing now, investigate thoroughly — keeping the good and throwing away the junk.

We will start with the study of evolution because that line of thinking seems to be the popular "trend" these days. Even some of the long-established church denomi-

The Earth — How Did It Come Into Existence?

nations are leaning toward some kind of evolution, because the evidence is so persuasive.

Before investigating the theory of evolution, we must have some understanding about three basic subjects. The first is SPACE and its magnitude. Second, TIME and its infinity. Third, LIGHT, that mysterious something the scientists have not been able to understand because *light* does not abide by any known physical law.

SPACE

Space cannot be understood by measuring it or by seeing it but by visualizing what is universally accepted as the truth. To have a better understanding what space is like let's go into empty space and investigate.

Let us suppose that space is limited in size with a wall around it; then look and see what is on the other side of the wall — just more endless empty space.

Logically, empty space always was — it had no beginning. Space is void of any substance and is totally dark. Would you say that we are still in the "dark ages" if it were claimed we are in the middle of space? Well we are and always will be. Since the Earth, sun and stars have come into existence they too are also in the middle of space. If we could travel at the speed of light for eternity we would still be in dead center of space. As big as our galaxy (Milky Way) is, it becomes an invisible speck compared to the vastness of space. It would be impossible to fill space with anything because it is unlimited. There would always be more room!

TIME

In the **far-long-ago** there was a period when time was not possible to calculate because nothing as yet came into existents to measure time by. There was not a

Day Six

beginning of anything to start calculating from! The Earth and Sun were as yet not formed so as to count days and years. So, millions or billions of years can not be used to denote the eons-gone-by. The only word that does have any meaning to describe the past is *eternity.*

To illustrate, let's draw a horizontal time line so we can visualize "eternity." It looks like this:

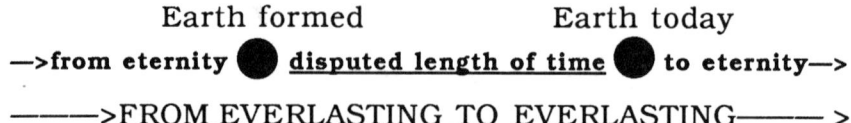

—————>FROM EVERLASTING TO EVERLASTING————— >

"Time," before anything came into existence, would be called eternity. And the future has no end. Thus we are in the middle of eternity never to come to the end of it. Eternity goes as far into the *past* as eternity will into the *future.* We will always be in the middle of eternity.

LIGHT

Scientists are confused about "light," because it does not abide by any known laws of nature. They assume that light travels on a mysterious substance that the scientists named "Ether." The encyclopedia gives this account of "ether."

COSMICAL ETHER

In physics and astronomy, postulated material substance, which is assumed to fill all space, and to *penetrate* freely among the ultimate particles of which all matter is composed. Although it has not been possible to determine the properties of the *ether of physics*, the admission of its existence

The Earth — How Did It Come Into Existence?

seemed a necessity of scientific reasoning. For we know that light is some kind of a periodic disturbance, and we know that it travels through interstellar space with a definite, finite speed. It appears absurd to suppose that a motion of any kind could take place in a void, in which there was nothing to be moved; and hence, as has been said, it appears to be a logical necessity to assume the existence of some kind of "luminiferous" (light-bearing ether) throughout space. . . . The mind cannot be brought to admit that it corresponds to the actual state of affairs in space. . . . We assume that the "ether" *penetrates* all bodies, ...
Encyclopedia Americana, book 10

"Ether" certainly does not fill space (nothing could fill endless space), but it could fill interstellar space. Several reputable physicists have formulated diverse theories as to what ether is, but none will hold up under scientific scrutiny.

At first it was thought to be an incompressible solid like "water" or maybe a jelly-like medium; but later reasoning was that could not be, because the moon, Earth and planets move through it freely without any apparent *friction*.

Now the physicists are of the opinion that **it is impossible** to form a theory that will describe the real properties of "ether." The latest theory of Maxwell states that "ether" must be "electro-magnetic."

We have a general picture of "time" and "space" before any physical substance existed, so we ask how did the scientists discover the way 'solid' material came into space? How did the sun, Earth, moon and all the stars and planets evolve into such an orderly, precise motion? So far, no theory has proven correct according to the known laws of nature — each has a fault that cannot be

Day Six

accounted for. We read in the encyclopedia how it was supposed to have happened.

> COSMOGONY, the term generally used to cover the theories or speculations concerning the origin and development of the various bodies or groups of bodies found in space. . . . Or briefly, cosmogony seeks to project this knowledge into both past and future so that we may infer how things began and how they will end, and, as far as possible, the intermediate steps. Or briefly, cosmogony describes the *evolution of the bodies* and systems which we study in astronomy.
>
> The **creation myths** of primitive peoples are *unscientific* attempts at cosmogony. The account of creation in Genesis is an excellent allegorical outline, the strong *evolutionary* tendency of which is usually overlooked. The Hebrews undoubtedly derived it from earlier and cruder ideas prevalent in the Euphrates Valley. . . .
>
> Cosmogony; *Encyclopedia*, book 8.

This material about cosmology is a very long explanation about the different theories of scientists on how the universe came into being. Most of those theories start with huge, whirling, hot gas which formed our sun and planets. Some say that everything in interstellar space was created in this manner. The gas exploded, with a **big bang**, forming the stars. None of the scientists have, as yet, any idea how the nebula of hot gas came into existence. This whole process is supposed to have taken about 3 billion years. I don't think any one of them was there to see it happen!

Let's consider the teaching of evolution and religion in public schools. Both sides want exclusive rights to

The Earth — How Did It Come Into Existence?

teach their own doctrine — no interference can be tolerated by either side. What is wrong with both sides sharing equal time? Better yet, why teach religion or evolution at all — learn it at home!

Schools are not for the purpose of teaching religion or evolution. Would a Mohammedan want his child taught Christianity, or Christian parents want their child to become an evolutionist. Schools are supposed to make people literate so that they can make a living in this topsy-turvy world.

It is not our intention to go into depth on the subject of evolution and religion, or "who done it." We will only *search* for the known truth — *truth that has stood up under thorough investigation.*

Day Six

marble. The geologist did not name each individual layer of rock, but bunched the layers into groups according to the fossils found or not found in them. The first group of strata was named Azoic or Archaeozoic because no fossils, of living things, have been found in this group of strata.

Reading from the book by H. G. Wells, *The Outline of History*: What Wells has written about geology and evolution contains the thinking of some of the most noted geologists of his time. He did extensive research work on the different theories of how life began on this Earth, and then wrote a book that was approved by geologists and evolutionists. It is written in such a convincing manner that you will believe it is **based on facts**. In his opening remarks he states:

> Astronomers give us convincing reasons for supposing that sun and earth and all the system were then whirling about at a speed much greater then the speed at which they are moving today, and that at first our earth was a flaming thing upon which no life could live. . . . They oblige us to believe that the sun, incandescent though it is, is now much cooler than it was, and that it spins more slowly now than it did, and that it continues to cool and slow down. . . . There was a time when the day was not a half and not a third of what it is to-day; when a blazing hot sun, much greater than it is now, must have moved visibly. . .from its rise to its setting across the skies. . . . It must have been in days of much hotter sun, a far swifter day and night, high tides, great heat, tremendous storms and earthquakes, that life, . . began upon the world.

Strata - Is it a Reliable Source of Information?

What evidence did the astronomers uncover that told them the Sun moved across the skies much faster than it does now? I cannot find it in print any place. How do they know that there were high tides, great heat, tremendous storms and earthquakes, when life began upon the world? Today we have earthquakes, and no life is generated. We have violent storms and great heat none of these conditions are conducive to life — in fact they destroy it.

The scientists have at their disposal laboratories that can duplicate any kind of weather conditions they want. The scientists also have chemicals that are most favorable to sustain life — yet they are not able to spawn the simplest form of life. If they did produce something that was similar to life, could it reproduce itself? Would it be able to find food and digest it? Life, even in the simplest form, is extremely complicated. Look up *cell* in an encyclopedia and you will find that a living cell is so intricately made that you will not be able to understand it.

In *The Oregonian* of January 20, 1980, there is an article written by Robert Locke about the Paleontologist, J. William Schopf. Mr. Schopf is examining a rock, taken from the Azoic stratum that is 3.76 billion years old, to find the very beginning of life on Earth. Schopf said,

> Nothing lived on that long-ago Earth. But the "oceans" were astir with promise's — they swirled and simmered a "primordial soup that held the raw materials of life." **Somehow**, probably in the first billion years of our worlds existence, that promise was fulfilled. A "nondescript glob of chemicals crossed some vague and wondrous boundary to become the first living thing.". . . [the] Earth eventually filled with a teeming diversity of life, from microbes to men. Still, . . . Man wonders who he is and where he came

Day Six

from and how he got here and how it all began.

When Schopf said, "nondescript glob of chemicals" he was telling us that he did not have any idea what the chemicals were. Take note how accurate he is with his figures. He does not round off his numbers and say about 3 billion years old; no, it's 3.76 billion years — not more and not less. Also, he states that the oceans were swirling with a primordial soup, the material that cells are made of.

This "imaginary soup'" is what he is trying to find. But he can't find it because there is no such thing as primordial soup. Scientists, as yet, have not found *organic carbon* on this Earth, the necessary element to produce living cells.

The gist of this search is to find some **organic carbon** that was in existence in this so-called primordial soup. Organic carbon comes only from "living things" — it cannot be manufactured artificially, and it does not exist naturally in the chemicals of the Earth.

Mr. Schopf knows that to produce a living cell requires organic carbon. He states that after living things came into existence from that primordial soup, for the first time, organic material was being produced biologically. But he has no facts or evidence to prove that the first organic primordial soup ever existed. He knows full well that a living organism could not originate from the chemicals of the Earth. So, he is trying to find some roundabout way that would make us believe it did happen anyway. From this imaginary first cell he runs the evolution chain clear through to man.

Another item we should examine, at this time, is in a newspaper article by George Alexander (*The Times-Washington Post* Service). It reads in part:

Strata - Is it a Reliable Source of Information?

OUR CONSTANTLY EXPANDING UNIVERSE

In fact, up until the 1920s, it was commonly thought that there was only one galaxy in the universe and that all matter that could be seen strewn across the skies was contained within our milky way system. . . from 1924 to 1934, . . . at the Hale Observatories — Dr. Edwin P. Hubble overturned that concept of the universe . . . . Today astronomers think they may provide answers to questions that have puzzled men for centuries, questions about the size and shape of the universe . . . . And then in 1924, Hubble presented the first concrete evidence that the universe and our galaxy were not one and the same thing. These findings, taken together with work done by astronomers at other observatories around the world, gave rise to the so-called "big bang" theory of the universe. According to this theory, the universe began as a super-dense ball of *energy*. The ball exploded — astronomers refer to this as the creation event — and the **energy was scattered, gradually becoming "matter"** as the universe constantly expanded. Today, using the 200-inch diameter telescope atop Palomar Mountain, a new generation of Hale astronomers believe they will soon be able to see the "edge" of the expanding universe. They may already be looking at it. Sir Arthur Stanley Eddington, British astrophysicist, had the best answer to that. He said that it was not correct to envision galaxies expanding into a space that was already there. Rather, *space itself,*

Day Six

expands, carrying the galaxies with it.

I have no remarks to make on this "big bang" theory because I was not there to see whether it happened that way or not. But it does stir up some questions. Where did that energy come from? Did it always exist? How did it form into a dense round ball, does just plain energy have gravity? Why didn't this energy turn into physical matter before it exploded. Consider this all happened in space that was void of any physical material. Would you give a passing grade to Sir Arthur Stanley Eddington, British astrophysicist, on his paper about "space expanding" and carrying the galaxies with it? How can endless space expand? The word *matter* as defined by *Webster's New World Dictionary* is this:

> 2. [matter] what all (material) things are made of; whatever occupies space and is perceptible to the senses in some way; in modern physics, matter and energy are regarded as equivalents, mutually convertible according to Einstein's formula, . . . (i.e, energy equals mass multiplied by the square of the velocity of light); in dualistic thinking, matter is regarded as the opposite of mind, "spirit," etc.

Einstein's formula certainly can not be applied here. Space contained no matter to form a mass, and there was no light to multiply the square of its speed.

Chapter 4

Mars and Strata

Nearly all evolution scientist believe that life existed on the planet Mars. In *The Sunday Oregonian*, March 1972, there was an article written by Marvin Miles, *LA Times-Washington Post* Service. It reads in part:

> Life on Mars? "Quite possible," says one of America's foremost planetary scientist. "Oversold," scoffs another. So far there is not a shred of positive evidence, n*or any definite negative evidence*, either, and this applies, as well, to all other bodies of the solar system, except the moon. But while there is a broadly controversial character to all available evidence, the search for life continues to intrigue many persons on the bases of its philosophical and *religious interest* as well as its technical and biological aspects. Dr. James Van Allen, University of Iowa scientist, . . . defines the issue: "Some persons suggest that the origin of living material is a kind of chemical, thermodynamically accident that — given the proper raw materials and physical conditions — can occur anywhere and probably has occurred at millions and millions of other sites in the universe." Allen explains: "A system

Day Six

is said to be living in the biological sense if it is capable of reproducing itself, using more rudimentary chemical materials as a starting point."

Dr. Bruce Murry, professor of planetary science at California Institute of Technology, says the imprint of astronomer Percival Lowell who at the turn of the century was intrigued by the possibility of crisscrossing canals on Mars, with "Oases" at interesting points. This in turn, suggested an intelligent Martin civilization, and the appeal of that possibility was too great for him.

This nonsense resulted from an overheated imagination that fogged his vision. **There are no canals**. As a result, he says, "Scientific opinion — while rejecting intelligent beings on Mars — **tended to accept uncritically** the likelihood of abundant plant life to explain the seasonal markings displayed by the planet. . . ." It is virtually impossible to prove the absence of an arbitrary, hypothetical life from Mars . . . Murry argues that not a single Mars observation to date has demonstrated organic constituents, much less biological ones. Murry notes that the **search for life has been a popular theme from the beginning.**

Now that it is a proven fact that there is no life on any of the planets, except the Earth, the scientists are sort of ridiculing those who believed there was. The truth is, many of the evolutionists believed life existed elsewhere. Now we have men coming to Earth in flying saucers from outer space.

The U. S. government, at great expense, sent a rocket

Mars and Strata

to the planet Mars **to find out if there was any** *life* **there now or any time in the past.** Also to determine if there is any *organic carbon* in the soil. The sole purpose, of this venture, was to find that life existed elsewhere than just on the Earth. The evolutionists continue to seek evidence to prove their theories.

In a NEWSPAPER article, before the rocket was launched, is Dr. Carl Sagan's opinion of the possible outcome of this costly venture of the Viking Rocket. The rocket was sent to the planet Mars for the sole purpose to search for any signs of life or organic carbon. Here is a report given in a newspaper:

> Dr. Carl Sagan, Cornell University astronomer, and one of the top planetary scientists in America, doesn't agree with his Caltech colleague on the. possibility of discovering life on Mars. He's excited about the *chances* for such a *profound discovery* — perhaps the most significant in history, *if it should occur* . . . . Thus Sagan is a strong believer in the Viking program *"to find out."* "There is a continuum of biological possibilities on the planet," he explains. "On one hand there could be no contemporary organisms, no signs of past life and no signs of pre-biologic *'organic' chemistry'* — **the stuff from which life arises.** On the other. hand, a whole spectrum of organisms might be found. Or perhaps there will be no signs of current life, but evidence of past life **without pre-biologic *organic* chemicals** — or maybe just these chemicals with no evidence of past or present life. . . there are those who say that if the Viking landers find no life, no signs of fossil life, not even any. pre-bio-logical 'organic chemistry,' the results will be of no interest. But that

23

Day Six

> a ***foundation of faith, that is systematically promoted.***"
>
> What is secular humanism? [It's a religion.] The most important belief of this religion is its denial of the transcendent and/or supernatural: ***There is no God,*** no creator, no divinity. Such a belief rest upon "faith." It is therefore, . . . **"a religious statement."** It is a curious thing: The ACLU . . . in defending the humanists, make precisely the same arguments when they are attacking the Baptists.
>
> Universal Press Syndicate.

This analysis and decision by Judge Hand pegs the theory of evolution as a religion based **not on facts** but merrily on the individual's belief.

STRATA ON THE SURFACE OF THE EARTH

Let's go now to the study of the rock strata that covers the entire Earth and see if we can find evidence that will prove any kind of belief.

We have to accept the fact that the Earth was formed somehow because we can see it! So, we will go on from this point and study the strata of the earth and the fossils they contain to see if there really is any evidence that proves evolution is based on scientific facts. To do this we will return to the book written by H.G.Wells.

> **We do not know how life began upon the earth.** Biologists, that is to say, students of life, have made guesses about these beginnings, but we will not discuss them here. Let us only note that **they all agree**

Mars and Strata

that life began where the tides of those swift days spread and receded over the steaming beaches of mud and sand. The geologists have divided the strata of the surface of the earth into *"six sections"* according to the fossils found or not found in them. The first strata has no fossils in it, (signs of life) so, they named it "Azoic" [meaning without life.] Overlying . . . these Azoic . . . rocks come others . . . which do contain traces of life.

These first remains are of the *"simplest"* descriptions; they are vestiges [traces] of simple plants, called algae, or marks like the tracks made by worms in the sea mud. This second series of rocks is called the Proterozoic *(beginning of life)* series, ...

According to Mr. Wells, only algae, possibly some tracks that could have been made by worms, have been found in these "proterozoic rocks." This is not the whole truth because the fossils of **all living things** are *fully developed* that are found in these rocks. A few pages later Mr. Wells states that:

In the case of most animals the new generation is on trial in a year or less. With such simple and lowly beings, however, as first appeared in the. primordial seas, growth and reproduction was probably a matter of **a few hours or even a few brief minutes.** Modifications and differentiation of species must . . . have been extremely rapid, — and **life had** *already* **developed a very great variety** of widely contrasted forms *before* **it began to leave traces in the rocks.** The Record of the Rocks does not begin, there-

Day Six

fore, with any group of loosely related forms from which all subsequent and existing creatures are descended. *It begins in the **midst** of the game*, with nearly every main division of the animal kingdom **"already represented."** Plants are already plants, and animals animals. The curtain rises on a drama in the sea that has already begun, and has **been going on for some time.** The. branchiopods are discovered already in their "shells," . . . . In the ocean waters, too, down to the utmost downward limit to which light could filter, **then as now,** . . . . But though the ocean and intertidal waters "already" swarmed with life, the land above. high-tide line was still, so far as we can guess, a. *stony wilderness* **without a trace of life.**

See how misleading this is. The "proterozoic" strata contains **all plants and animals** that exist on the Earth today, and they are fully developed.

Proterozoic, which means "beginning of life," is certainly misused here. Fossils found of *plants*, fish and animals are already fully developed as they are today. Some animals do not have skeletons, such as the jelly fish and worms, but still they are found as fossils in these rocks and are not just tracts or vestiges.

A very important question is: Why did some plants and fish go from the warm steaming beaches down to the far depth of the ocean to live, where it is cold and dark? The theory of evolution is that sea life sought to climb out of the water onto dry land where the sun was bright and warm. But the abundance of plants and fish in the deep, cold, ocean waters prove that this is not the whole truth.

Did the plants and trees also climb out of the ocean, and cross the dry beach sand to live on the rocky dry

Mars and Strata

land? Maybe there were "two primordial soups"; one on the hot steamy beach, and one on the dry land. Maybe a "nondescript glob of chemicals crossed some vague and wondrous boundary" to become the second beginning of living things? Mr. Wells writes:

> So far as we [geologists] can guess the dry land was a stony wilderness; not a trace of life. Why? If there was an ocean, there certainly was rain on the land. If there was rain, there certainly were pools of water and rivers and swamps. These pools and swamps all had different nondescript globs of chemicals washed in by the rivers — also plenty of mud. This second glob of nondescript chemicals would be safe from the sea's violent storms and pounding waves. The pre-biologic chemicals could, perhaps, brew into "organic carbon" from which all "living" things consist.
>
> Now reflecting on the strata that covers the Earth, the impression we get is that this strata lay in uniform order like the pages in a book (1,2,3,etc.). Number one on the bottom, and on up to page six at the top. Unfortunately that is not the case. We will again refer to Mr. Wells' book. He explains the condition of these rock layers that contain fossils. "These markings and fossils in the rocks and the 'rocks themselves' are our first historical documents. The history of life that men have puzzled out and are still **puzzling** out from them is called the Record of the Rocks. By studying this record men are slowly piecing together a story of life's beginnings, ... But when we call these rocks and the fossils a record and a history,

Day Six

it must not be supposed that there is any sign of an orderly keeping of a record. It is merely that what ever happens leave some trace, if only we are **intelligent enough to detect the meaning of that trace**. Nor are the rocks of the world in orderly layers one above the other, convenient for men to read. They are not like the books and pages of a library. They are torn, disrupted, interrupted, flung about, defaced, like a carelessly arranged office after it has experienced in succession a bombardment, a hostile military occupation, looting, an earthquake, riots, and a fire.

Notice that he said "what ever happens leaves a trace" so why didn't the beginning of life leave a trace before it was fully developed? Because the strata is in such a jumbled-up mess, no wonder the pathologists and geologists do not agree with each other. One could say, "I think this torn page belongs to the middle of page one" and the other would answer, "No, that is part of page three," and so, on and on.

Should we believe the guessing of those who are prejudiced, and are only searching for evidence to prove their theories? The normal way would be to find the evidence first, and then from this evidence, [**with intelligence**] form an opinion of what the evidence indicated. Not concoct a **conclusive theory first**, and then search the world over for evidence to prove it to be correct.

The geologists and astronomers have given their scientific estimate on how many millions of years have passed from the beginning of the universe until now. Lets see how accurate they are, or, maybe how careless. We will again read from Mr. Wells:

Mars and Strata

Speculations about geological time vary enormously. "Estimates" of the age of the oldest rocks by geologists and astronomers starting from different standpoints have varied between 1,600,000,000, and 25,000,000. The lowest estimate was made by Lord Kelvin .... Professor Huxley "guessed" at 400,000,000 years. ... It must be clearly understood by the reader how sketchy and. provisional all these time estimates are. **They rest nearly always upon theoretical assumptions of the *slenderest kind*.** ... It is quite open to the reader to divide every number ... by ten or multiply it by two; **no one can gainsay him.**

Can one believe the professional, expert geologists and astronomers when they give the geological 'time' as a scientific "fact"? They do not agree with each other by millions of years.

Supposing one multiplies the 1,600,000,000 by ten that gives 16,000,000,000 and then divide the 25,000,000 by ten. The difference in their estimate is beyond reason. This is allowed, and nobody can gainsay it because none of the evolution experts have any knowledge or proof about the age of the Earth.

Chapter 5

Piltdown Man

It would not be proper to talk so much about evolution and not say something about the dinosaur, those ferocious, reptilian animals of such gigantic size. Some of them were so huge that their legs were not strong enough to hold them up on dry land, and therefore they had to stay half submerged in water and mud for support.

It seems that the evolutionists have decided that birds evolved from dinosaurs. We have been misled somewhat — all dinosaurs were not so big; some were as small as rats, and none were as big as the whales that are alive today. Under the heading *Dinosauria* in the *Encyclopedia Americana* there is an article that reads:

> A group of reptilian animals which flourished during the Mesozoic Era . . . possessed a more or less scaly or armored skin and were probably cold-blooded . . . . It was assumed that they were egg-laying, and the discovery of many dinosaur eggs in Mongolia in 1925 proved this to be a fact.
>
> In their anatomy the dinosaurs show certain features which link them with the birds . . . [the] *bipedal running* on the part of dinosaurs and birds and the consequent modification of the hind limbs, these similarities of structure also imply genetic or

blood relationship.

The dinosaurs, at any rate such as are known to us, were inhabitants of the lowland lying along the shores of the seas and ocean sand. Some were actually partly, if not wholly, water-living, although none show an extreme of adaptation to aquatic life and none were salt-water inhabitants, the occasional inclusion of their remains in marine strata being the result of accident.

It seems very strange that there is no evidence of dinosaurs until the Mesozoic strata, and then, all at once, these huge monsters appear. The Mesozoic is the fifth period of geological era, in which rock strata and fossils form a definite sequence. It is also strange that these dinosaurs do not show any adaptation to aquatic life if all living things came out of the ocean. They were living in swamps, but had no aquatic features. I wonder what kind of *accident occurred that put some in marine strata?*

MAN

Finally we come to the Cainozoic strata (the sixth), the Age of Man and Mammals. Man is the pinnacle of all evolution — **THE BRAIN! and also, the super duper!**

The evolution scientists have had a difficult time trying to prove their theories concerning the beginning of the Universe, but now, they claim to have the proof of man's evolution. In various parts of the world, bones have been found that scientists say indicate man did evolve from the monkey. In other words, man's great-great grandfather was a monkey; and we can take the monkey's word for it.

Day Six

A type of primitive man lived about 477,000 years ago in China, his fossil remains were found near Peking in 1929. He was named "The Peking Man.".Other fossil remains were found in Germany, called the "Heidelberg Man." But the fossil found in England was the most important of all the others, *(according to English scientists),* and is named the Piltdown Man. An account of this discovery is recorded in the *Encyclopedia Americana.*

Piltdown Man (Eoanthropus dawsoni)

Some pieces of a human cranium and a part of a lower jaw found in ancient river gravels at Piltdown in Sussex, England, in 10 11-1912, have evoked more controversy and a more legitimate difference of opinion than any other discovery relating to early man. The cranial fragments are essentially those of Homo Sapiens, their most remarkable feature being their unusual thickness, but the lower jaw, consisting almost of the complete right half and containing two molar teeth, is strikingly apelike in the chin region (which has a well-marked "simian shelf" as in **recent** manlike apes), and somewhat so in the form of the molars, so apelike, in fact, that **had it been found "alone,"** it would undoubtedly have been considered the jaw of a *"fossil ape."* . . .

Sir Arthur Smith Woodward, convinced that the Piltdown jaw belonged with cranium despite its apelike character, united these fragments to constitute the type of a new genus and species, Eoanthropus (dawn man) dawsoni.

Piltdown Man

The association of jaw with cranium as a single type received apparent confirmation from a second discovery in 1915, some two miles from Piltdown, in which a lower molar, practically identical with the corresponding tooth in the famous jaw, was found with some cranial fragments very like the original skull. Unfortunately, "theological age" of the Piltdown **gravels is somewhat uncertain,** though competent opinion now places them as Early Pleistocene. Many authorities believe the skull to have belonged to a later period and to have become accidentally mingled, perhaps during a freshet, with older gravels and **fossils of various ages.**

The proponents of the Dawn man theory hold, on the other hand, that the Piltdown cranium is not Homo sapiens but a vastly older perhaps ancestral type, an early hominid in which the brain (about 1,240 cubic centimeters) had developed far in advance of the jaws which had not yet progressed beyond an apelike ancestral condition.

It may be said, in general, that the circumstance of the discovery tend to support the validity of Eoanthropus, but the fact remains that the association of the apelike jaw with a cranium essentially of Homo sapiens type seems grotesquely incongruous. *"British authorities"*... accept the **authenticity of the Dawn man.**

Apparently, the geologists cannot tell the exact age of fossil bones. Rather, they rely on the strata the bones are imbedded in. They cannot estimate the age of these bones, because the gravel has been mixed up with older

Day Six

gravel. If they are uncertain about the age of the bones, how can they judge the age of the gravel? One thing, *all agree*, is the fact that the **jaw bone is a fossil** buried for 600,000 years and that the skull is that of early man.

Geologists and biologists have been searching all over the world for the so-called missing link between man and animals. Some are now certain that the Piltdown fossil proves that man evolved from the ape because of the **ape-like fossil jaw bone.**

These bones were so precious an underground vault was built to preserve them forever. Only plaster copies are on view for the public to see and believe. **Now, evolution could be classed as a science!**

In the November.22, 1953, issue of the *Los Angeles Times* was another article about the Piltdown man.

PILTDOWN MAN BRANDED AS FAKE

Three British scientists cracked down on the Piltdown man today as an unscrupulous hoax. And for 40 years, they declared, the Piltdown man has been making *monkeys* out of anthropologists with the jaw bone of an ape. Someone had put over the most **outrageous fake** in paleontological annals, they said. Charles Dawson, attorney and amateur antiquary, dug the Piltdown relics out of a Sussex gravel pit between 1911 and 1913. After a few initial doubts many anthropologists hailed them as a "historic pointer" to man's early history — the practically complete skull of a dawn man who stalked the earth 100,000, to 600,000 years ago.

The *Encyclopaedia Britannica*, with reserve as to some discrepancies, has called the "relics" the second most important known to science, beaten only by "Javanese" **"missing link"** turned up in **1891**. "The discovery at Piltdown," it said, "shows that race of mankind had come by a brain that had reached human estate and that this race still retained certain definite simian characteristics in its jaws, teeth and face." Simian' was the right word, according to the information today from Dr. K. P. Oakley of the British Museum and Oxford University Profs. J.E.Weiner and W. E. le Gros Clark. They reported up-to-the-minute chemical tests prove **beyond doubt** that the vital jaw bone of Dawson's discovery was a **"deliberate" plant faked up from the skull of an ape.** That ape . . . was a modern ape that died an untimely death at 10. The ape's jaw bone and its canine tooth found with it . . . had been artificially stained to match the appearance of skull *fragments* found earlier. In addition the tooth had been artificially pared down to disguise its original shape. . . .

The Piltdown man has been recorded with varying degrees of acceptance in encyclopedias, books on anthropology and other reference works for many years. The investigators said the cranium itself still stands as a genuine fossil. But they put its age at 50,000 years, half the previous widely held minimum.

Why do you suppose these scientists perpetrated a hoax like this? Trying to dupe people into believing something that is not true is the worst kind of lie and apparently even many anthropologists were fooled — or were they?

Day Six

What kind of faith can we have in scientists who can't tell a fossil from a fresh bone? Here was a fresh jaw bone to examine and they concluded, without any doubt, that it was 600,000 years old. Some did have the intelligence to suspect, a little, that it was still more like a simian jaw, but they joined it to a small piece of cranium bone (probably an artificially stained human skull) and thereby **"discovered" the "dawn man."**

Let's read what H. G. Wells wrote about prehistoric man in his book *The Outline Of History*:

> One group of creatures is of peculiar interest in a history that is mainly to be the story of mankind. We find fossils in the Eocene of monkeys and lemurs, but of one "particular" creature we have as yet — ***not a single bone.* It was half ape, half monkey;** it clambered about the trees and ran, and probably ran well, on its hind legs upon the ground.
>
> It was small-brained by our present standards, but it had clever hands with which it handled fruits and beat nuts upon the rocks and perhaps picked up sticks and stones to smite its fellows. **It was our ancestor.**

That is a darn good description of early man, considering that scientists do not have a **"single bone" to go by.** Wells forgot to mention that this early man's eyes were blue!

If there was only "one" accidental cross between a monkey and an ape, then how did it multiply in order to throw stones at its fellows? It takes two **("male and female")** to multiply. If it is common for monkeys and apes to cross breed, why not experiment today with monkeys and apes to see how the human race began?

Piltdown Man

Maybe later there, must have been, another accidental cross that produced a **superior female?** The female is much farther advanced in the line of evolution than the male. **The male still has the "old- fashioned outside plumbing."**

It is strange that only parts of skull bones have been found, *never any bones of the face.* Why haven't they uncovered some leg bones to see how an ape's legs changed to that of Man, so that it could walk upright?

Let's return to the Piltdown episode and consider something that allegedly happened. The Piltdown ape "met an untimely death at the age of 10". How did they know that? Some one must have had inside information from the zoo where the apes were kept. "Untimely death" must mean the ape was killed to get its jawbone. If the theory of evolution is the truth, the scientists killed one of their ancestors; perhaps their great-great grandfather.

We have read enough to prove that those who claim evolution is a *"science"* have no evidence to prove that it is a science.

Just for fun, we will read an article that is in the current news and see what the scientists of evolution have been doing in the **past century.**

Less then one hundred years ago there were two scientists who were strong rivals in the science of fossils, especially which one would find the largest dinosaur. O. C. Marsh was America's first professor of paleontology, and E. C. Cope, was head of the Hayden Survey. The article reads in part:

> Actually, the dinosaur battle started in 1869 when Cope made a mistake in restoring remains he received from Kansas of a giant creature with a long name commonly known as the "ribbon reptile." The skeleton

Day Six

was arranged in the Museum of the Philadelphia Academy of Natural Sciences. There, Marsh noted that parts of the long vertebrae were **reversed.** Marsh taunted Cope in print. Cope retaliated. . . .
By Phil F. Brogan, *The Oregonian.*

It doesn't make sense that one who is an educated pathologist could be so careless or ignorant to put part of the vertebrae in backward. This was the beginning of a long struggle between these two scientists to find the first and biggest dinosaur. The same rivalry exists today. Some of the evolutionists today are striving to find the **bones of the "missing-link" first.** What are the odds? I would say they are 100 to 1 none will find it!

Chapter 6

Fossils

It seems that some scientists (those who believe in evolution) are rivals with each other. Each one wants to be the first to discover the biggest, or maybe, the oldest fossil. They also find fault with each other's work, and also are envious of each other's theories and discoveries.

No love is lost. Frequently, in the newspapers, one may read an account pertaining to the theories of evolution. Some of these articles are reviews by science writers in order that the layman may understand what the scientists are doing and thinking about. Here is a clipping of interest written by Warren E. Leary.

3-MILLION-YEAR-OLD BONES RAISE PEKING MAN DOUBT.

A newly discovered skull of an early ancestor of man raises "doubts" about the dating of the famous "Peking Man fossils," *anthropologist Richard E Leaky* said . . . the complete skull **he uncovered** last year in northern Kenya is an "estimated" 1.5 million years old, yet is almost identical to fossils found near Peking dated at only a half-million years. Fossils so alike should be from creatures that. existed at about the

Day Six

The fish named "Coelacanth" (pronounced see-la-kanth) is given this great honor because of the shape of its fins. These fins are extended from its body by short **limbs.** Scientists therefore theorize that these limbs became the four legs found on all land animals. This fish has two more leg-like fins on its back.

This is the way the evolutionists explain how this fish left the ocean: it would walk out of the water (with its leg-like fins) onto the beach for short periods of time. Finally, it developed lungs to breath air, and stayed on the warm land, **never going back to the ocean.**

Just recently, the Coelacanth has been discovered to be still *alive* — **it is not extinct.** This procedure, (of crawling out of the water) is entirely impossible because the Coelacanth lives at great depth in the water, about 650 to 2,000 feet deep, and never comes near the shore; not only that, it cannot stand sunlight and dies within a few hours of exposure. Therefore this fish could not have come up out of the dark, deep water and walk on the dry hot sand, and still live. Only about 28 Coelacanth have been caught so far because of the great depth of water they live in.

If the Coelacanth is a living fossil, then so are all the other animals, because they too left fossils behind them at the same time in the same strata of rock. The only difference is: the scientists thought some animals were extinct, so, dated these fossils millions of years in the past. Now, much to their chagrin, they are finding out that **some are still living.** So, to save face, are calling them "living fossils.".

The scientists say that the reason these living fossils have not made any improvement in these past millions of years is they reached the end run of evolution — **they were already *perfect.*** Mother Nature and Father Time could not make any more improvements. If so, how could any animal evolve from the Coelacanth if this fish had reached the end run of perfection?

Another newspaper article is about the evolutionists' theory of the development of subhumans to that of humans. In this article is an **artist's drawing** of five subhumans. The picture shows them walking one behind the other. The first subhuman, starting from the left, is named Sivapithecus (17 million years old). The second is five million years. The third is three million years, and then it shows Homo Habilis, two million, and Homo Sapiens, thirty-five thousand years. The only change that is noticeable is: they keep getting taller and the arms get shorter! The last two are intelligent enough to carry a long stick for a weapon. All five of them are naked — that is, they have no fur to keep them warm.

For millions of years man's ancestors must have had a miserably cold existence without fur to keep them warm. Perhaps they had a thick skin like an elephant to keep them warm, or a heavy layer of fat as the hippopotamus.

The broken rocks that the geologists claim to be man's first tools certainly were not adequate enough to tailor skins into a covering to keep him warm.

Man is not covered with fur, to keep him warm, so he must have evolved from the hippopotamus. This surely must be a scientific fact because I have seen people that looked just like a hippopotamus, and some are very thick-skinned.

See how new theories can originate and become a scientific fact. When theories are proven wrong they still remain in the scientific journals the same as some of our outdated laws remain in the law books. An example of this is contained in an article written by Phillip Whitteen in the *Parade Magazine* of Oct. 28, 1979:

> DINOSAURS! The largest creatures ever to walk the face of the earth. Yet dinosaurs

Day Six

> — literally, "terrible lizards" — have always suffered from an image problem in the public mind. Though they ruled the earth for more than 140 million years, we have thought of them as plodding, pea-brained, cold-blooded reptiles.... Recently, however, paleontologists (scientists who study fossils) have begun to reevaluate our most cherished beliefs about the dinosaurs and have come up with some startling conclusions. These new ideas may explain not only why the dinosaurs dominated the planet for so long, but also *why they disappeared so suddenly*. Moreover, at least some and possible all dinosaurs were **warm-blooded** — more like today's mammals and birds than like reptiles. Perhaps most startling of all is the assertion that not all the dinosaurs died out some 65 million years ago. One line lives on today. We call them birds.

I wonder if it could have been the other way around — dinosaurs evolving from birds? Feathers are a very complicated thing to develop on a creature that is already covered with fur or scales. Maybe the ostrich (with two toes), or the rhea (with three toes) was the start of the dinosaur. Maybe they dropped their feathers, or plumes, then began to grow hair. (Once I saw a **fan-dancer drop her feathers, and that sure raised more then eyebrows!**) The article continues,

> The hunting behavior of Deinonychus — and a similar dinosaur discovered later in the Gobi Desert of Mongolia with its claws embedded in the underbelly of a smaller, plant-eating dinosaur — led Ostrom [a sci-

Living Fossils

entist] to suspect that some dinosaurs might have been warm-blooded. Robert T. Bakker, a paleontologist at Johns Hopkins University, has become the most outspoken champion of the warm-blooded dinosaur theory. Not all paleontologists "accept" his views, but Bakker believes that all dinosaurs except the earliest were warm-blooded. Studies have shown that when warm and cold-blooded animals compete for a habitat, the "warm-blooded" animals — mammals and birds — win out. *"**Mammals** and **dinosaurs*** first evolved at about the same time." Yet for **tens of millions of years,** the dinosaurs held sway over the earth, while our own rat-sized ancestors huddled fearfully in the nooks and crannies to avoid their foes. If endotherms are superior to ectotherms, Bakker wondered, why didn't the early mammals win out? Could it be the dinosaurs, too, were warm-blooded?

I don't think the temperature of animals had anything to do with survival of the species. We have cold-blooded animals and fish today that survive in abundance. Some warm-blooded animals kill to eat and some live on vegetation, the same pattern continues with the cold-blooded ones. The animals that live on vegetation are harmless, but meat eaters kill the harmless for food. When the food is gone, all die. What prevented the warm-blooded mammals from holding their own against the dinosaurs? At that time there were saber-tooth tigers; huge bears and all the rest of the animals of today.

The warm-blooded whale does not compete for his habitat, but, never-the-less, whales will soon be extinct because man wants their fat and oil. $.$.$.! MONEY,

Day Six

MONEY, MONEY.
If the dinosaurs lived for tens of millions of years and all of a sudden vanished from the face of the Earth, it was not the warm-blooded mammals that killed them because these warm-blooded mammals also, **vanished at the same time.** Continuing the article.

> Although there seems to be an enormous gap between birds and reptiles, the British biologist T.H. Huxley first suggested more than 100 years ago that birds evolved directly from dinosaurs. He proposed as the first bird a little fellow known as Archaeopteryx, or "ancient feather," whose fossil remains — clearly showing its feather covering— .... Archaeopteryx was an almost-perfect half-bird, half-reptile. Smaller than the smallest dinosaur it was about the size of a crow — it had wings and feathers like a bird, but it also had teeth and the skeleton of a reptile. Like all birds, Archaeopteryx had a clavicle, or wishbone. But no dinosaur had ever been found with a clavicle, so the gap between dinosaur and bird remained. . . . In the past few years, however, dinosaurs with wishbones, including John Ostrom's sickle-taloned Deinonycchus, have been found. Most scientists now agree that Archaeopteryx, or some similar creature, was indeed the first bird. It had feathers which were used not for flying but mainly for **"insulation."** Only warm-blooded animals are insulated, either with feathers or hair.

The theory of evolution has no "indisputable facts." Therefore, "logic and reasoning" are the only tools the scientists have to work with. When a fossil is found, much logic and reasoning has to be put into the study of it, to determine what class of animal it is, and also, what kind of animal evolved from it. Some of the scientists do not agree with each-other's analysis. Therefor, it looks like the scientists are not using the right tools — Logic and reasoning.

According to the scientists, animals that are warm-blooded are insulated with hair or feathers to keep them warm. Man has warm blood, so, he also should be insulated with hair or feathers. On man, hair is not used to keep him warm, therefore man did not evolve from an ape. He is in a class all his own — *"A naked savage"!*

Part II

Creation

Chapter 8

Is There a God?

Those who believe in evolution have not given us any undisputable facts. So now let us see what the Fundamentalists and man-made religions have to offer?

It is logical to ask: Why do we need a religion? Was religion conceived by the governments to control the people? Is it possible there really is a Living Spirit known as God? We know that outer-space had no beginning and was totally void of any substance whatever, so, how could there be a God? If by chance *there is a God*, why did He wait so long (billion of eons) to create the earth? According to the "Hebrew Scripture" God only worked for six days and then took a day off to rest, never to work again. How and where can one find information on this subject?

I suppose the logical place to find the answer to these questions is to go to the **original source — the *Hebrew* Bible.** But first we must learn something about that Bible in order to understand it.

THE HEBREW BIBLE

Not all religions are based on the written word found in the Hebrew Bible. Those who believe that the Bible contains *the exact Word of God* are called fundamentalist. Those who read the Bible do not always interpret the

Day Six

things written therein as having the same meaning, such as William Jennings Bryan did in the so-called "monkey trial." He interpreted *each day* (of the first seven days) to be twenty-four hours long.

In the beginning of the history of man, all important historical events were kept in memory by commemorating certain feast days. At that time people lived an extremely long life. They were able to tell the history of past events orally to many generations. This method of recording history was used until the time of Moses, then he put this past history in writing. Today the Bible is a compilation of the history of events and writings of prophets up to the time of Jesus (known as The Old Testament). Then the Apostles kept record of events according to a New Testament.

The Bible is a recognized authority that priests and ministers base their doctrines on. To see how reliable and trustworthy these *doctrines* or religions are it is necessary to go to the Bible and read it for ourselves so that we can check it out against their beliefs.

Most of us do not know much about the Bible and the things written in it or why it was written. We will have to read and study the Bible ourselves in order to find the answer to — *are these man-made religions* based on the **truth**?

It would be a big relief to know, *for sure*, if what is written in the Bible really is the truth, or just a well thought-out fable!

Most everyone who has a **specific form of religion** tries to make others believe as they do. This search will not advocate any particular form of religion, but point out some of the untruths. We will *investigate and question* — **but not believe.**

We will determine *(according to the Hebrew Bible)* if there is a **living God**? If so, how did this God come into *existence*? **How old is this world and the universe?**

Is There a God?

Also, what is *light,* that mysterious substance named "ether"? We will also try to find out what happened to the dinosaurs that caused them to disappear so suddenly?

This is going to be a long, hard job. I hope you, the reader, will have patience enough to read to the end.

The truth is hard to come by because of the many lies that fool us. **We also fool ourselves by having such strong, *fixed beliefs*,** so that we cannot recognize the truth when it is found. We are all so **cock-sure that what we already believe is the truth.**

Searching for the truth can be compared to a prospector seeking gold.

He may be standing in a place were there is gold all around him but still cannot find it because he does not recognize it. Many times a prospector will load himself down with iron pyrite, which looks like gold, but is only fool's gold. If the prospector would hit the fool's gold real hard it would fall apart, but no, the prospector lugs it for miles thinking he is rich, only later he finds out he has nothing for all his labor.

Now let's go on searching and try not to get loaded down with fool's gold. We will hit every thing real hard to see if it falls apart.

MANY RELIGIONS

There are many different kinds of religions in this world; some that believe in one god, and others that believe in many gods. Some who worship statues, rocks and paintings (that have fallen down from heaven), spiritualism, witchcraft, voodoo, black magic, and some even worship the devil.

In the Orient are some very old religions, and also some that are fairly new. The primary ones are Buddhism, Confucianism, Hinduism and Mohammedanism.

Day Six

If we tried to include all these religions in the search for the truth we would certainly get bogged down with fool's gold. So, only three religions will be examined that base their belief on the words of the prophets, written in the Hebrew Bible. These three are: (1) The Jewish religion (over 2,600 years old) which forms the basis for the other two. (2) The Catholic Church. (3) The Christian religion, originally known as **"The WAY,"** which is less than 2,000 years old.

We will not investigate very deeply into the religious doctrine to try and prove that any one of them is right, that is up to the individual to decide.

We will only search out the false doctrines the theologians are teaching which are "man-made" religions.

We cannot recognize the mistakes in religion until we find out: **Is there a God? Why do we "*need*" a religion?** After we learn something about these questions then we will be able to criticize the *man-made* religions.

We will now search to see **if there really is a God; a Living God that is mentioned in the Hebrew scripture.**

IS THERE A GOD?

We started out in the vast, dark, empty space when investigating cosmology. So again, we must go out into empty space and look around to see if we can find anything we missed. We must travel back into the eons of time, before the Earth came into existence. We must search farther back than that, we must go into eternity.

We are now in empty space looking in all directions but see nothing — because nothing existed. We are in cold, total darkness. We have gone too far back into eternity so we must skip ahead to a period known as **"from eternity."** Again nothing can be seen. If there really was something there to be seen our eyes would not be able to see it anyway, because there is no *ether* there for light to travel on.

We must put on a pair of **"mystical glasses"** so that we can see in the dark, and also can see the *invisible*. But these mystical glasses will not work with ordinary eyes. They can only be used for our mind's eye. Now with our mind's eye we see a bright light. This bright light is so huge it goes beyond our eyesight and also our imagination. It seems to be in motion, and drawing together — it is taking some kind of form that cannot be recognized because of its extreme size.

How long it takes for the forming of this luminous invisible something is not possible to determine. The time it took can only be expressed as *from eternity*. The scientists do not have a name for this luminous, invisible light because most do not believe it ever existed. In the Hebrew Bible the prophets have given a name to this light — they called it ***"The Living Spirit."***

The statements I just made about the invisible luminous vapor only sets an **imaginary** *scene* to give us something to discuss and investigate.

TIME AND SPACE

Time had no beginning. It goes back into the "past eons" the same as the future will go into eternity. Thus we are in the middle of time.

The same thing applies to *space* — it has no boundaries. Space is endless in all directions. It would be impossible to fill space, with anything, because there would always be more room.

Therefore it would be impossible for the, so-called, Living Spirit to fill space because space is endless. Also the Living Spirit could not be from the beginning because

Day Six

there was no beginning. So it can't be said, The Living Spirit always was.

Let's stop theorizing and ask the one who knows. We will ask the Living Spirit Himself when and how He came into existence and take His word for it.

But I find we do not have the personal contact, with the Living Spirit, to ask such a question. But the Living Spirit has already told us about His beginning. The Living Spirit, speaking through His prophet Isaiah, said to the *Hebrews*:

> "You are My *witnesses*. . . . In order that you may **know and believe** Me, and understand that I am He. ***Before Me*** there was no God **formed,** and there will be none after Me. I, even I, am the Lord; and there is no *savior* besides Me. . . . So you are My witnesses, declares the Lord, And I am God. Even ***from eternity*** I am He. . . . I am the *first* and I am the last, and there is no God besides Me."
> Isaiah 43:10-12

I believe this is written so clearly that no one can give the wrong meaning to it. God is talking to the Hebrews and telling them that He has chosen them as "witnesses" and that He wants them to understand who He is — the only God, the first and the last — their savior. There was no God *FORMED* before Him, and He has control so that there will not be another spirit FORMED in the future. He does not claim to have always existed, but says that He is FROM ETERNITY.

In Isaiah 44: 6,8 God confirms it again to be sure the Israelites understand.

> Thus says the Lord, the King of Israel and

Is There a God?

his redeemer, the Lord of hosts: I am the **first** and I am the **last,** and there is no God besides Me.... Is there any God besides Me, or is there any other Rock? I know of none.

Evidently God took no chances, He searched for some time in space to see if there could have possibly been another spirit. Then said, "I know of none." In other translations the word *Rock* is translated *God.* In Isaiah 48: 12 we read:

"Listen to Me, O Jacob, even Israel whom I called; I am He, I am the first, I am also the last."

This is not a theory — we have the written word in the Hebrew Bible. There is no guessing; we have a positive statement in written history.

When God said, "I am the first, I am also the last" that indicated that there was a possibility of another spirit, but none could be found. The question now is, after the Spirit was formed, how did the spirit obtain the knowledge to *create the world* and the universe and be capable of putting living things on the Earth? His wisdom and power are declared to be infinite. How did He get this wisdom and power?

Solomon, (another prophet of God) reputed to be very wise, tells us how God obtained this knowledge. He tells us how the Spirit obtained this *wisdom that gives Him* **power.**

Chapter 9

The Personification of Wisdom

King Solomon, the son of King David, was a very wise man. Solomon was an inspired prophet (according to the Hebrew scripture). He wrote the book called Proverbs, in which he strongly recommends everyone to obtain wisdom for his own good. In the Book of Proverbs he **personifies Wisdom** as an intelligent individual. Wisdom then tells how God gained His knowledge so that He was capable of creating everything that now exists. Wisdom now speaks to us — .

> Does not *wisdom call, and understand ing lift up her voice* .... "To you, O men, I call, and my voice is to the sons of men. . . . I, wisdom, dwell with prudence, and *I find knowledge and discretion.*"
> Proverbs 8:1, 4, 12

In the King James translation it reads: "I wisdom dwell with prudence, and find out knowledge of **witty inventions.**" This gives a better understanding of how the Spirit gained His knowledge and understanding — **"by witty inventions."**

"Counsel is mine and sound wisdom; I am understanding, *power* is mine. . . . **The Lord possessed** me at the beginning of His way,

The Personification of Wisdom

before His works of old. **From everlasting I was established,** *from the beginning,* **from the earliest times of the earth. When there were no depths I was brought forth, . . . While He had not yet** *made the earth* **and the fields, nor the first dust of the world. When He established the heavens, I was there, when HE inscribed a circle on the face of the deep . . . When He marked out the foundations of the earth; then I was beside Him, as a master workman; and I was daily His delight, rejoicing always before Him, rejoicing in the world, *His earth,* . . . ."**
Proverbs 8:14, 22-27, 29-31

The Living Spirit did not start to work as an apprentice or an unskilled workman without any plans or a blueprint. The Spirit first sought knowledge about the vast space He was in. God sought to know if there could possibly be another Living Spirit like himself — He found none.

Living in empty space was not too desirable. So the Living Spirit began to study — wisdom was constantly by his side — and by witty inventions He discovered how to create the elements. He then worked up a detailed plan how to create things that would be for *His own pleasure.* He arrived at a plan that He was capable of and powerful enough to perform no matter what happened, or, what went wrong. The time it took for The Spirit to gain this complete, detailed knowledge of everything can only be stated as part of eternity. When His plans were complete in the most minute detail, the Living Spirit was ready to go to work!

For the Living Spirit to build (or create) the Living Spirit had to have material to work with. Most ministers and priests lead us to believe that all the Spirit had to do was to say, "Let there be" and presto there it was. Or,

Day Six

maybe the word was hocus-pocus?

There is no denying that solid material came into being some way, because we are here; and can see the moon, stars, and the things about us. How did they come into being? We will have to search this question out by using a little reasoning, **some modern-day science,** as well as the Word written in the Bible.

Apostle Paul, who was reputed to have a little extra knowledge and understanding of the word of God, explained to us what the world was made out of.

> By faith **(belief)** we understand that the worlds were prepared by the *word* of God, so that what is seen was not made out of things which are visible.
>
> Hebrew 11:3

There are many things that are invisible such as: air, electricity, radio waves and sound. Is it possible that material things were made from any of these? To answer that question we must go to the one who performed this task — the Living Spirit.

One of God's favorite prophets was King David, who wrote in the Book of Psalms how God created substance.

> To Him who rides upon the highest heavens, which are from ancient times; behold, He speaks forth with His voice, a **MIGHTY VOICE."**
>
> Psalms 68:33

This statement gives the location ("highest heavens"), and the time ("ancient times"). So, this took place out in space before the creation, and it was a **MIGHTY voice.** This description sets it apart from other times when God has spoken softly. *Spoken* indicates the use of words like

The Personification of Wisdom

(Let there be), but *voice* means the sound of the vocal cords. In this case there was a blast of a **MIGHTY VOICE** that EXERTED ENERGY. Now there was energy in space.

Scientists state that energy and matter are *interchangeable*. That is, energy can be converted into substance or substance can be changed to energy. So, this *mighty voice* that produced this energy really produced **ELECTRONS and PROTONS**. This is similar to the Big Bang theory that the scientists claim was the beginning of substance. By this mighty voice, that sounded with spoken words such as "Let there be," the space that is called "Stellar Space" was filled with dust. Now the Living Spirit had plenty of material to work with to start creating all that He had planned.

We must now come to an understanding of the words *Living Spirit* and *God*. First the Living Spirit was formed — we have not been told what a spirit is, nor in what form. The Spirit became a God to man after man was created.

In this study we are relying on the Jewish prophets, who were inspired by the God of the Hebrews. Starting from the very beginning of Genesis we read about God's work in creating.

THE CREATION

> In the beginning God created the **heavens** and the **earth**.
>
> Genesis 1:1

The way this reads, the Spirit first created a place for Himself, which is called heaven. You might say heaven was an office for the Spirit to work from or a Throne Room for a king.

Then the Spirit forms the Earth. The Spirit gathers a

Part III

Religion

Day Six

> proceeded forth and came from God; neither came I of myself, but he sent me. Why do ye not understand my speech? even because ye cannot hear my word. Ye are of your father the devil, and the lusts of your father ye will do. He was a murderer from the beginning, and abode not in the truth, because there is no truth in him. When he speaketh a lie, he speaketh of his own: for he is a liar, and *the father of it*. And **because I tell you the truth, ye believe me not."**
>
> John 8:42-45

Who is this person Jesus is referring to when he says, "the devil is your father?" In the *Reader's Digest Thesaurus* "FAMILY WORD FINDER" the word *devil* is explained like this:

The Devil. Exploring the word:

> The Devil slanders God and righteousness — his name comes from Greek *diabolos*, slanderer, backbiter. *Satan* comes from Hebrew *Satan*, enemy. *Lucifer* comes from Latin *lux* (light) + *ferre* (to bear). light-bearer.

There are still more names given to Lucifer such as: Beast, Serpent, Snake, Beelzebub, Baal, Angel of Light, King of Tyer, etc. Because the devil is given these different names the people don't realize that it is Lucifer who is fighting against God and causing so much trouble on this Earth.

The Bible contains the history of man from Adam and Eve to the very end of all the physical material of God's creation. But woven into this history is the word of God,

History of Man and Signs Given to Him

how God is going to defeat and destroy his enemy Lucifer. This information is scattered throughout the whole Bible, but it takes much searching to find it.

When God questioned Adam and Eve about their unbelief and the eating of the fruit, Adam blamed Eve for giving him the fruit. Eve blamed the serpent for deceiving her. Then God cursed the serpent and said,

> "I will put enmity between you and the woman *between your seed and her seed*; **He** shall bruise you on the head, and you shall bruise him on the heel."
>
> Genesis 3:13

It is plain to see that from the woman's *seed* some man would come to fight Lucifer, and bruise Lucifer's head. Since man has fallen into the hands of Lucifer, Lucifer is *man's father*. Any woman who becomes pregnant from the sperm of man — gives birth to a man that is really the seed of Lucifer. **Finally there was a one who was born from a woman, that had not become pregnant by man.** This man was called the **Son of Man and also the Son of God.**

Each generation kept hoping, watching and waiting for this promised Son of Man to come and fight the battle with Lucifer. No definite time was ever given as to when this would happen.

To show how man had been waiting for this promise to be fulfilled we read what they hoped and expected of Noah when he was born.

> When Lamech had lived a hundred and eighty-two years, he became the father of a son, and called his name Noah, saying, "Out of the ground which the Lord has cursed this one shall bring us relief from our work and

Day Six

from the toil of our hands."
                                    Genesis 5:28

Man was expecting the fulfillment of the promise God gave to Eve, that her seed would bruise the serpent's head and the curse would be removed, so that man would not have to earn his food by the sweat of his brow. Man did not understand how or when it would come about, but was always expecting and living in hope.

Man wanted to return to the Paradise he had once known and lost. The human race wanted to escape the curse of death. But for some reason man was (and is) more interested in the pleasures of this world than he is in God. Man still doesn't believe the word of God written in the scripture; he always theorizes in his mind a religion that suits him better.

Before the flood, man lived for eight hundred years and more which made it possible for a few very strong leaders to become wicked, greedy kings. They made slaves of the people of the world. Man became so violent and greedy that God decided to destroy all living things from the face of the Earth with a flood. He would then start over again with His plan to populate the Earth.

After the deluge Noah lived three hundred and fifty years, almost until Abraham. So by Noah and his three sons, the history of the flood was well known.

Lucifer soon deceived the new generation into worshiping false gods. So God chose Abraham, a Hebrew, to be the progenitor of a *peculiar* people. Peculiar because they, as a race of people, would believe in only one God and be His witness.

Their ceremonies were to be a sort of pantomime acting out God's plan to pay the price for man's redemption from the curse of death and to finally destroy Lucifer.

Prophets (by the spirit of God) would tell the Jews in

detail of the coming *seed of Eve*, who would also be the son of God. These "peculiar people" would also be witnesses of God's power and willingness to "forgive" the sins of those who **believed**. Now let it be understood these people were "chosen" by God to serve Him — it was not the descendents of Abraham that made the choice.

Abraham's grandson was given the name Jacob. God renamed him Israel which became the name of the whole nation. These peculiar people belonged to God, and if at anytime they went astray God would punish them as a father would chastise a son, so that they would obey His word.

Because God had chosen a people as His very own, this caused some kind of violation with Lucifer's privileged authority. After all, man belonged to Lucifer — Lucifer was their father. So God had to concede some kind of compromise. This is written in Isaiah:.

> . . . But now thus says the Lord, he who created you, O Jacob, he who formed you, O Israel: **"Fear not, for I have redeemed you;** I have called you by name, you are mine. . . . For I am the Lord your God, the Holy One of Israel, your Savior. *I give Egypt as your ransom, Ethiopia and Seba in exchange for you.* Because you are precious in my eyes, and honored, and I love you, **I give men in return for you, peoples in exchange for your life.** . . . *Bring forth the people who are blind, yet have eyes, who are deaf, yet have ears!"*
>
> Isaiah 43:1, 3-4, 8

I presume that every one knows the history of Jacob and his family living in Egypt for many generations, finally becoming slaves. God sends a great

Day Six

These signs that are given to the Hebrews to watch for are clues, so the chosen people will be able to recognize the son of man when he comes at the appointed time.
Another clue given by Isaiah:

> The people who walk in darkness will see a great light; those who live in a "dark land,'"the light will shine on them. . . . For thou shalt break the yoke of their burden and the staff on their shoulders, the rod of their oppressor, ... For a child will be born to us, a son will be given to us; and the government will rest on His shoulders; and His name will be called Wonderful Counselor, Mighty God, Eternal Father, Prince of Peace. There will be no end to the increase of His government or of peace, on the throne of David and over his kingdom, to establish it and to uphold it with justice and righteousness from then on and for evermore. The zeal of the "Lord of hosts" will accomplish this.
>
> Isaiah 9:2,4,6-7

This is addressed to the people who are in darkness, which indicates that the people or generation at the time this prophesy will be fulfilled will be a people that do not understand the plan of redemption, or recognize the fulfillment of this sign. But a light will be given to those who are willing to listen. He will break the yoke of their burden, that is, the strict laws they are under.

"For a child will be born to us." This will be the fulfilling of the promise Moses spoke of: "The Lord your God will raise up for you a prophet like me from among you, from your brethren — him you shall heed." Who is this son? We just read that a virgin was to bear a son,

History of Man and Signs Given to Him

and his name was to be Immanuel. Again Isaiah says his name will be called "Wonderful Counselor," that is he will teach the people how to really serve God. Another name is "Mighty God," Because he is God's son he is equal to God. He is also of royal blood, a descendant of King David. In His Kingdom, He will sit on David's throne and be king of the chosen people.

King David also prophesied a great deal about the son of man and how that son continually prays to his father to save him from the curse of death. This son falls under the curse of death because he assumes the guilt of all the sins of man, he will die — be sacrificed — for the sins of all mankind. Here is one of His prayers.

> O god of my praise, do not be silent! For they have opened the wicked and deceitful mouth against me; They have spoken against me with a lying tongue. They have also surrounded me with words of hatred, and fought against me without cause. In return for my love they act as my accusers; but **I am in prayer.** Thus they have laid upon me evil for good, and hatred for my love. . . . But thou, O God, the Lord, deal kindly with me for thy name's sake; because Thy lovingkindness is good, deliver me; for I am afflicted and needy, and my heart is wounded within me. . . . My knees are weak from fasting; and my flesh has grown lean, without fatness. I also have become a reproach to them; when they see me, they wag their head. Help me, O Lord my God; **"save" me according to Thy lovingkindness.** And let them know that this is Thy hand; thou Lord, haste done it.
> Psalm:109

The prophets — by the Spirit of God — gave the Jews

Day Six

Jesus, but, they were unable to prove any to be true. While they were shouting these accusations, Pilate brought out Jesus after he had been beaten and tormented by the Roman soldiers. The Jews did not recognize Him because He was so badly "disfigured." So Pilate called to the Jews, **"Behold your King!"** Isaiah prophesied this event many years earlier when he said,

> . . . so His appearance was marred more than any man, and His form more than the sons of men.
> Isaiah 52:14

Then Jesus was nailed to a cross and became accursed for all mankind as it has been written: "Cursed is every one that hangeth on a tree." Galatians 3:13

This wooden cross was really a symbol of the "tree of knowledge of good and evil" that caused the fall of man. All these things were seen by many witnesses.

Chapter 12
Misinterpretation of the Dove and The Rock

Fundamentalists are those who believe the Bible word for word. They do not take into consideration when or where the event took place; who was speaking or to whom, or analyze the true meaning of the words.

If the Bible is going to be read for the information contained therein, it certainly seems proper to only accept the words for their true meaning. When reading the Bible, you must try to understand what the scripture *positively* means. To understand what is written in the Bible takes only a little common sense.

As an example, most fundamentalist believe that the Spirit of God looks like a dove because the Bible said so. An example is needed here to illustrate how some of the fundamentalists misinterpret the scripture.

One day John, the Baptist, saw Jesus coming to him to be baptized, and said:.

> "Behold, the Lamb of God who takes away the sin of the world? This is **He** on behalf of whom I said, 'After me comes a *man* who has a higher rank than I, for He existed before me.' And I did not **recognize Him,** but in order that He might be manifested to Israel, I came baptizing in water." And John bore witness saying, **"I have beheld the Spirit descending as a dove out of heaven,**

Day Six

and **He** *remained upon Him.* And I did not recognize Him, but He who sent me to baptize in water said to me, '**He** upon whom you see the Spirit descending and remaining upon Him, this is the one who baptizes in the Holy Spirit.' And I have seen, and have borne witness that this is *the Son of God.*"
John 1:29-35

Did you take note that the word *as* was used to describe how the Spirit descended on Jesus? And did you notice that a capital *H* was used on the pronoun *He* to denote the gender? If John was still speaking about the dove he would have used the neutral gender *it*.

Many churches picture the Spirit looking like a dove and have a picture of a dove on the altar to represent the Spirit of God. John, the Baptist, did not say the Spirit looked like a dove, but that it *descended* like a dove. The dove flies to and hovers over the place where it wants to land and then descends straight down. If John was writing this today, he probably would say "the Spirit descended like a helicopter." So the Spirit did not look like a dove, but descended like a dove, and *"remained on him."* Let's read again how John spoke about the Spirit descending on Jesus but this time leave out the part about the dove descending.

"I have beheld the Spirit descending out of heaven, . . . and He remained upon Him."

A serious mistake some fundamentalists are making about this *dove problem* is that they are breaking the commandment of God by using the picture of a dove to represent the Holy Spirit. Read what God commanded Moses while he was on top of the flaming Mount Sinai.

Misinterpretation of the Dove and The Rock

> Then God spoke all these words, saying, "I am the Lord *your* God, who brought you out of the land of Egypt, out of the house of slavery. You shall have no other gods before Me. *You shall not* make for yourself an 'idol,' or any *likeness* of what is in heaven above or on the earth beneath or in the waters under the earth. You shall not 'worship' them or 'serve them,' for I, the Lord your God, am a **jealous God, ...**"
>
> Exodus 20:1-5

God certainly does not want man to use anything on Earth to represent Him, nor to share any of His glory. The Living Spirit is invisible, no man has ever seen Him to know what he looks like. Jesus, God's son, said he saw the Father but did not describe His form, only His quality: **light; loving kindness, and willingness to forgive.** Later, Jesus was asked by His Apostles to show them the Father. Jesus answered,

> "Have I been so long with you, and yet you have not come to 'know' Me? He who has seen Me has seen the Father; how do you say, 'Show us the Father'? Do you not believe that I am in the Father, and the Father is in Me? The **words** that I say to you I do not speak on My own initiative, but *the Father abiding in Me does His works*. Believe Me that I am in the Father, and the Father in Me; otherwise *believe on account of the works themselves*."
>
> John 14: 9-12

So you see, God does not look like a dove or anything else on this earth. Jesus said, "He who has seen me has

Day Six

seen the Father." God declares that He is invisible, so all that we can see are His "works," and hear His word. Jesus said, "I am in the Father, and the Father is in me." Therefore Jesus, the Son of Man, is the "temple" of the Invisible Spirit. So the Father is in Jesus' body of flesh which God prepared for Himself to abide in, in order to partake of the pleasures of His creation.

An outline of a *fish* is seen on the front of many pulpits to symbolize God. Apostle Paul declares:.

> For since the creation of the world *His invisible attributes*, His eternal power and divine nature, have been clearly seen, being understood through what has been made, so that they are without excuse. For even though they knew God, they did not honor Him as God, or give thanks; but they became futile in their "speculations," and their foolish heart was darkened. **Professing to be wise, they became fools,** and exchanged the glory of the incorruptible God for an image in the form of *corruptible man* and of birds and four-foot animals and crawling creatures. Therefore God gave them over in the lusts of their hearts to impurity, that their bodies might be dishonored among them. For they exchanged the *truth of God for a lie, and worshipped and served the creature rather than the Creator.*
>
> Romans 1:20-25

I think this statement, by Apostle Paul, makes it clear that those who use or worship an object (thinking it represents God) become fools — by fooling themselves.

Another example of how some of the fundamentalists misinterpret an important Scripture that most church-

Misinterpretation of the Dove and The Rock

goers believe in, especially the Catholics. The Scripture concerns the Apostle Peter and the rock on which Jesus said He would build His Church. This is a very serious mistake because it takes the authority from God and gives it to man.

The word *church* was not referred to in the Old Testament, and in fact was not used in the whole Roman World. Jesus was the first to use the word *church* while teaching the people about the coming of the Kingdom of God. The Hebrews did not have a church, but had a temple in Jerusalem and synagogues in most all towns. The Roman Empire had shrines for the many gods of their liking. These gods usually came in groups of threes (Trinity).

Both the Hebrew and Roman religions were state religions. Their religion was the government. The Roman Rulers were given the title of *pontifex maximum*, that is, the **head bishop of Rome and of the pagan religions of the whole world.**

The Hebrews, at first, had God as their king but soon changed to having a man rule and plunder them as all the other nations. The Law and the words spoken by the prophets were gradually changed to the thinking of fundamentalism.

This was the condition of the world when Jesus spoke to the twelve Apostle about building his "Church on the Rock."

Apostle Matthew writes about this conversation:.

> Now when Jesus came into the district of Caesarea Philippi, He began asking His disciples, saying, **"Who do people say that the Son of Man is?"** And they said, "Some say John the Baptist; and others, Elijah; but still others, Jeremiah, or one of the prophets."

Day Six

He said to them, "But who do **you** say that *I am*?'" And Simon Peter answered and said, "Thou art the **Christ,** the Son of the living god."

And Jesus answered and said to him, "Blessed are you, Simon Barjona, because flesh and blood did not reveal this to you, *but My Father* who is in heaven.

"And I also say to you that you are Peter, and upon this rock I will build My church: and the gates of Hades shall not overpower it.

"I will give you the *keys* of the **kingdom of heaven;** and whatever you shall bind on earth shall be bound in heaven, and whatever you shall loose on earth shall be loosed in heaven."

Then He *warned* the disciples that they should tell no one that **He was the "Christ."** From that time Jesus Christ began to show His disciples that He must go to Jerusalem, and suffer many things from the elders and chief priests and scribes, and be killed, and be raised up on the third day.

And Peter took Him aside and began to rebuke Him, saying, "God forbid it Lord? This shall never happen to You."

But He turned and said to Peter, "Get behind Me, Satan. You are a stumbling block to Me; for you are not setting your mind on God's interests, but **man's."**

Matthew 16:13-34

It is clear that the *first subject* of this conversation is: "Who am *I*?" It is not about the church that is to be built. The answer was given by Peter, "Thou

Misinterpretation of the Dove and The Rock

art the *Christ*, the Son of the living God." Then Jesus said, "Blessed are you, Simon Barjona, because flesh and blood did not reveal this to you, but My Father who is in heaven."

When Peter said you are "the Christ" then Jesus in return said, "I also say 'you are Peter.'" This is the end of this short subject.

Then a new subject is discussed. This time it is about the rock? *(Thou art the Christ),* the Church is to be built on. Jesus then states that on this rock *(Jesus is the Christ)* I will build **My church** and He warned the apostles they should not tell anyone that **He was the Christ.** The subjects about: the Christ, the rock and the church is ended.

While the twelve apostles and Jesus were indulging in private conversation on various subjects, Jesus began to explain to them how He must suffer from the elders and chief priests and be killed and then raised up on the third day.

So Peter took Jesus to one side and said to Him? "God forbid it, Lord! This shall never happen to You."

Then Jesus turned his back to Peter and said, "Get behind Me, Satan! You are a stumbling block to Me; for you are not setting your mind on God's interest, but man's."

Now let us do some honest reasoning; do you suppose that Jesus, after calling Peter "Satan" and a stumbling block and not having God's interest but his own, would chose Peter as the foundation rock to build His Church on? Jesus the *"Christ"* is the foundation rock on which the church was to be built!

To support this line of reasoning consider how Mark reported this same incident:.

"Who do people say that I am?" and they told Him, saying, "John the Baptist; . . . ."

Day Six

The Jews recognized Jesus as an ordinary man, they knew his family and his brothers and sisters. Jesus was certainly not the type of man the Jews had visualized to be *the "Christ."* They were expecting some one like King David to sit on David's throne, a great warrior, able to free them from the Romans. That is why the Jews could not believe Him to be "The Christ." Not only that, the Jews were expecting the Christ to be from the city of David, not from Galilee!

The Jews did not understand that the promise given to them was: the **Christ was to be like Moses —** *meek and humble.* Jesus **the Christ, who was the Rock,** turned out to be a rock the Jews stumbled over.

The Apostle John begins his Gospel by explaining the spiritual side of Jesus. Apostle John reveals to us what and who Jesus really was:

> **In the beginning** was the **"Word,"** and the Word was with God, and *the Word was God.* He [the word] was in the beginning with God. All things came into being by Him, and apart from Him nothing came into being that has come into being. *In Him was life,* and the life was the light of men. And the light shines in the darkness, and the darkness did not comprehend it (Or, overpower it).
>
> John 1:1

Jesus said that He spoke only what God told Him to say. This reveals that Jesus was the **word** of God. We have already shown how all things were created by the **word of God** — with a mighty voice. Therefore all things were created by the word of God, which was now in the body of the son of man. In the Son was life, and He came as the Christ (the anointed one) to give life to man. Jesus also was the light given to man by showing man how to please God — by believing in the truth, that is, Jesus is the Christ.

The answer to the "second question" is a little more difficult. If God was so willing to forgive man of his sins why not just forgive and have it over with instead of making a body of flesh and blood for His Word to dwell in, and then suffer the pains of death? God must have had no **alternative.**

A decision in most all legal questions is based on a precedent case that serves as a guide. So let's search for a precedent case that shows us why God had to have a son to accomplish **His work.**

THE PRECEDENT CASE

Saul, of the tribe of Benjamin, was the first king of Israel. He disobeyed God, so God did not permit any of his sons to inherit the Kingdom. So then David, of the tribe of Judah, was anointed king with the promise that his kingdom would last forever.

Many years later, David's son, Absalom, plotted with the Tribe of Benjamin to overthrow his father in order that he would become the king.

King David fled from the city of Jerusalem with several hundred of his loyal friends. King David's escape from his son, Absalom, is told in the second book of Samuel:

> When King David came to Bahurim, behold, there came out from there a man of the family of the house of Saul whose name was Shimei, the son of Gera; he came out cursing continually as he came. and he threw stones at David and all the servants of King David; and all the people and all the mighty men

Day Six

> were at his right hand and at his left. And thus Shimei said when he cursed, "Get out, get out you man of bloodshed, and worthless fellow! The Lord has returned upon you all the bloodshed of the house of Saul, in whose place you have reigned; and the Lord has given the kingdom into the hand of your son Absalom. And behold, you are taken in your own evil, for you are a man of bloodshed!"
>
> Then Abishai the son of Zeruiah said to the king, "Why should this dead dog curse my lord the king? Let me go over now, and cut off his head."
>
> But the king said, "What have I to do with you, O son of Zeruiah? If he curses, and if the Lord has told him, 'Curse David,' then who shall say, 'Why have you done so?' . . . So David and his men went on the way; and Shimei went along on the hillside parallel with him and as he went he cursed, and cast stones and threw dust at him.
>
> 2 Samuel 16:5

Absalom with his soldiers, followed King David across the Jordan river, and there they met in battle. Absalom was killed, and the revolution ended. So then David began his return to Jerusalem with all his household. Here is the narrative:

> Then "Shimei" the son of Gera, the Benjamite who was from Bahurim, hurried and came down with the men of Judah to meet King David. And there were a thousand men of Benjamin with him, . . . and they rushed to the Jordan before the king.
>
> Then they kept crossing the ford to bring

Jesus, The Way

over the king's household, and to do what was good in his sight. And Shimei the son of Gera fell down before the king as he was about to cross the Jordan.

So he said to the king, "Let not my lord consider me guilty, nor remember what your servant did wrong on the day when my lord the king came out from Jerusalem, so that the king should take it to heart.

"For your servant knows that I have sinned; therefore behold, I come today, the first of all the house of Joseph to go down to meet my lord the king."

But Abishai the son of Zeruiah answered and said, "Should not Shimei be put to death for this, because he cursed the Lord's anointed?" David then said, "What have I to do with you, O sons of Zeruiah, that you should this day be an adversary to me? Should any man be put to death in Israel today? For do I not know that I am king over Israel today?" And the king said to Shimei, "You shall not die." *Thus the king swore to him.*

2 Samuel 19:16-23

Many years later when King David was old, and about to go as all flesh he appointed his son Solomon to be king. **King David put everything under his son's rule** saying:

"And behold, there is with you Shimei the son of Gera the Benjamite, of Bahurim; now it was he who cursed me with a violent curse on the day I went to Mahanaim. But when he came down to me at Jordan, I swore to him

Day Six

> by the lord, saying, 'I will not put you to death with the sword.'
>
> "Now therefore, *do not let him go unpunished,* for you are a wise man; and you will know what you ought to do to him, and you will bring his gray hair down to Sheol with blood."
>
> 1 Kings 2:8

Here was a situation where King David could not take revenge on his enemy because he had given him a promise, under oath, not to kill him. But now things were different; everything was now under the authority of his son Solomon, who is not under obligation to anyone. So the thing to do now is to have Shimei disobey King Solomon so that the king could have cause to kill Shimei. The trap was set like this:

> Now the king (Solomon) sent and called for Shimei and said to him, "Build for yourself a house in Jerusalem and live there, and do not go out from there to any place. For it will happen on the day you go out and cross over the brook Kidron, you will know for certain that you shall surely die; your blood shall be on your own head." Shimei then said to the king, "The word is good. As my lord the king has said, so your servant will do."
>
> 1 Kings 2:36-38

After three years Shimei did cross the brook Kidron. He went after two of **his servants that ran away;** he brought them back the same day. This violation of the agreement he had with King Solomon gave Solomon the right to have Shimei cut down with the sword.

Jesus, The Way

We now have a precedent case that shows us why God needed a son in order to destroy Satan — God's ancient enemy. Jesus, the son of man, took on himself all the sins of the world, and thereby was subject to death. Satan then was able to have him crucified — he belonged to Satan. But God loved his son and raised him from the dead. The trap was set.

Satan followed Jesus to heaven to claim Him as his own. The Son was to be the **Temple of God** so Satan would not take **no** for an answer. Satan and his angels started to fight, but the angels of God overpowered him and cast him to the Earth. Now he could never again enter heaven to accuse man of sinning. Lucifer's head was bruised.

Here we need some authentic Scripture to support this statement about Lucifer, (Satan or devil), having his head bruised.

The Apostle John had a vision of coming events to the very end of God's plan. Being this was a "vision" it is written with symbols that must be translated for what they represent. The trouble is, some theologians interpret the symbols, in this vision, to substantiate their beliefs.

This is the way it is written with some abridgment of remarks not pertaining to this subject:

> And a great sign appeared in heaven: a woman clothed with the sun, and the moon under her feet, and on her head a crown of twelve stars; and she was with child; and she cried out, being in labor and in pain to give birth. And another *sign* appeared in heaven: and behold, a great red dragon having seven heads and ten horns, and on his heads were seven diadems. . . . And the dragon stood before the woman who was

Day Six

> about to give birth, so that when she gave birth he might devour her child. And she gave birth to a son, a male child, who is to rule all the nations with a rod of iron; and her child was caught up to God and to His throne . . . . And there was war in heaven, Michael and his angels waging war with the dragon. And the dragon and his angels waged war, and they were not strong enough, and there was no longer a place found for them in heaven. And the great dragon was thrown down, **the serpent** *of old* **who is called the devil and Satan, who deceives the whole world;** he was thrown down to the earth, and his angles were thrown down with him. . . . Woe to the earth and the sea, because the devil has come down to you, having great wrath, knowing that he has only a short time.
>
> Revelation 12:1-12

The Devil, in his wrath, was now going to try and destroy the Church built on the Rock, **by changing his pagan religion to a Christian "copy" of the church (called The Way) corrupting it from within.** At the same time Satan would torture and kill the ones who believed in the **Christ** — trying to make them deny Jesus. Satan continues to cause many real believers, who will not deny their belief in the Lord Jesus, to be slain.

We should discuss the meaning of some of the symbols, shown in the vision, so that we understand alike.

The woman that is about to give birth to a son symbolizes the Hebrew Nation (the Israelites). The crown of twelve stars are the twelve tribes that make up the nation of Israel. The pain of birth is the anxiety the Jews were having concerning the Christ who was to come. The moon and sun are symbols of pagan superstition that was always amongst them.

Some religious denominations interpret the woman to be the Virgin Mary and the crown of stars making her the queen of heaven.

Lucifer, in arranging to have Jesus nailed to the cross, bruised Jesus' heel. When Lucifer was cast out of heaven and confined to the Earth, never again able to rise from the Earth to enter heaven, his **head** was bruised.

ACTS

The book of Acts contains the story of the beginning of The Church called ***The Way,*** and the struggle the church had. Lucifer was now desperate because he now knew his time of survival was short. His only chance to survive is to destroy the Church built on the Rock. At first, those who had faith in Jesus were at a loss, not knowing what to do because Jesus had returned to His Father. A large group of believers were with the Apostles in a large room praying:

> These all with one mind were continually devoting themselves to prayer, along with the women, and Mary the mother of Jesus, and with His brothers.
> Acts 1:14

Is it reasonable to ask, why were his brothers there praying? His brothers did not believe that Jesus was the promised Messiah. In the Gospel of John it reads:

> His brothers therefore said to Him, "Depart from here, and go into Judea, that Your

Day Six

> disciples also may behold Your works which You are doing. For no one does anything in secret, when he himself seeks to be known publicly. *If You do these things,* show Yourself to the world." For not even His brothers were believing in Him.
>
> John 7:3-5

The reason Jesus' brothers were there with their mother was that they were younger and still under the rule of their parents.

The Jewish law at that time was that the children did not become of age until they were thirty years old, therefore they must do as their parents directed or be punished by that law.

By the genealogy of the Jews, Jesus was heir to David's throne. After Jesus was crucified, James, his brother, became the next in line to the throne. The Romans did not like anyone to be a king, over a nation, other than the emperor of the Roman Empire. So the emperor of the Roman Empire (who was the Pontifex Maximus) later made James a bishop of Israel. James was not a Christian bishop, but a bishop of the Catholic pagan belief, because the Roman religion at that time was pagan.

Since James was appointed bishop of Israel by the Emperor Nero, who was Pontifex Maximus, James had control of both Jewish and Roman religions that were in his given territory — the see of Israel. *"See"* is a Catholic Church word which means a definite boundary of territory governed by a bishop.

Even though **James did not believe in Jesus,** he was, nevertheless, the leader of the Christian religious movement that was called *The Way* because he was now the Bishop of Israel. Even Peter and Paul, and all the other Apostles, had to get an ok from James on anything they wanted to do.

Jesus, The Way

The Apostles were afraid of Bishop James because he had Roman soldiers to enforce his commands. James hated Paul because he had gone over to the Gentiles and was teaching the plan of salvation to them, without first making them Jews by circumcision. Apostle Paul tells of an encounter with James:.

> But when Cephas (Peter) came to Antioch, I opposed him to his face, because he stood condemned. For prior to the coming of **certain men from James** he used to eat with the Gentiles; but when they came, he began to withdraw and hold himself aloof, **fearing the party of the circumcision**. And the rest of the Jews joined him in hypocrisy, with the result that even Barnabas was carried away by their hypocrisy.
> But when I saw that they were not straightforward about the truth of the gospel, I said to Cephas in **the presence of all,** "If you, being a Jew, live like the Gentiles and not like the Jews, how is it that you compel the Gentiles to live like Jews?"
> Galatians 2:11-14

Since James had the authority of bishop, let's search and see where this title of bishop came from. The Catholic writers try to downgrade the office of bishop by saying it means *presbyter*. The Jews never had a bishop in their religion, it comes from the Roman pagan worship. **It seems that information about bishops has been destroyed,** so we will have to *search with our eyes open* and use some common sense.

In the *Encyclopedia Americana*, under the title" bishop," is found information to use as a starting point to find out were the word *bishop* came from and what it really meant.

Day Six

BISHOP . . . The name was *borrowed* by the first Christians from the languages of Greece and Rome, in which it designated a **civil magistrate.** Thus, Cicero was at one time [episcopus orae campaniae]. In the New Testament the words *bishop* and *presbyter*, or *priest*, are sometimes interchanged, ... Yet, as maintained by *Roman Catholic writers*, it does not follow because the names *priest* and *bishop* were then applied "indistinctly," that there existed no distinction between the episcopate and the priesthood. "There might have been confusion in the names," says Saint Thomas, "but not in the character." The identity of the *original signification* of the words *presbyter* and *bishop* was acknowledged by the Christian fathers Saint Jerome and Saint Augustine in the 5th century, and even by Pope Urban II at the end of the 11th century, and it is not denied by many Episcopalians even at the present day.

Volume 4:14

The definition of the word *episcopate* that is mentioned a few lines above.

WEBSTER'S NEW WORLD DICTIONARY

e.pis.co.pate. . .1. the position, rank, or term of office of a bishop. 2. a bishop's see. 3. bishops collectively.

So the name *bishop* was borrowed from the Romans

Jesus, The Way

and meant "civil magistrate." That certainly indicates who ever was called a bishop had authority over every religion in his given territory or "see."

We just read that Cicero, a well-known statesman, orator, and Stoic philosopher, was a bishop. He lived more than 45 years before Jesus was born, therefore at that time a bishop could not have been a Christian, but had to be a worshiper of Roman pagan gods. That reveals to us that James, who also was made a bishop the same as Cicero, was a Catholic who worshiped all pagan gods. Or at least, if James believed in only one God as the rest of the Jews, he was, nevertheless, the civil magistrate of the Roman Catholic pagan religion.

While Bishop James, brother of Jesus, was Bishop he wrote an open letter to the twelve tribes of Israel. The **"twelve tribes"** comprised the *whole nation of Israel.* The "twelve tribes" certainly were not believers in Jesus — they are the ones that had Jesus crucified. Bishop James really did not say anything of importance in his letter to the twelve tribes, but he did try his best to contradict Paul's teaching of salvation by **faith,** that is, **believing Jesus is the Christ. Very few fundamentalists understand what Bishop James really was trying to tell the Jews when he wrote that open letter. This is part of the letter:**

> ...You have *condemned and put to death* the righteous man; he does not resist you. *Be patient,* therefore, brethren, until the coming of the Lord.
>
> Behold, the farmer waits for the precious produce of the soil, being *patient about it,* until it gets the early and late rain. *You too* **be patient;... for the coming of the Lord is at hand.**
>
> James 5:6-7

Day Six

It clearly shows here that James did not believe that Jesus was the promised Lord — the Christ. He is telling the twelve tribes that the righteous man (Jesus) did not resist you. To have patience the Lord will soon come. The Jews, to whom Bishop James is writing this letter, did not believe Jesus was the "Christ" and for them to be patient — the Lord would soon come.

The twelve tribes of Israel believed that the promised one would never die as Jesus did. Not until Jesus rose from the dead did a few of the Jews believe.

The Caesars of Rome had the title of Pontifex Maximus, that is, each one of the Caesars at the time he reigned was head of the Catholic religion, and these pontiffs appointed bishops all over the entire world. Julius Caesar and also Caesar Augustus had the title of Pontifex Maximus, and they reigned long before Jesus was born, therefore, the bishops they appointed could not have been Christians — they were Catholic pagans — worshipers of all the known gods.

Before Jesus, there was no religious persecutions because there was no church for Satan to destroy.

Here is another article about bishops in the *New Americanized Encyclopedia* (which is a very old issue) under the name of "EPHOR." It reads in part on page 2282:

> EPHORI. This name, *meaning bishop* or overseer, was given to certain magistrates in many Dorian cities of ancient Greece. But the most prominent are the ephors of Sparta, who, whatever may be their origin, appear during the time of which we have "historical knowledge" as the **"supreme power"** in the state, controlling alike its civil and military administration. When, in the third century B.C., the complete humiliation of Sparta led

the kings Agis III and Cleomenes III to resolve on restoring what they supposed to be the ancient constitution, their first blow was directed at the "ephors," whom they charged with deliberate usurpation.

This we must consider: a bishop is a "civil magistrate" of the Roman government. The name *bishop* has been used by other religious denominations because the world has been dominated for so many years by the Roman Catholics. The title *Bishop* [civil magistrate] was in use many years before Christianity.

After many years, when the Christian doctrine became well known, many of the Roman Citizens began to be interested in this *new religion*. But the Catholic bishops taught the citizens of the Roman Empire that Jesus was another "god" and to add Him to their many deities.

At this time of world history the Emperor was no longer civil ruler (that power was returned to the Senate). The Emperor now only had the authority to enforce the laws made by the Senate. But the Emperor remained the Pontifex Maximus.

According to the history given by Eusebius, Pilate sent word to Emperor Tiberius about Jesus. It reads like this:

> And in accordance with an ancient custom that those who were ruling over the nations should report to him who held the imperial office any new movement among them, in order that no event might escape his notice. Pilate communicated to the Emperor Tiberius the story of the resurrection from the dead of our Savior Jesus as already famous among all throughout all Palestine,

Day Six

> together with the information he had gained of his other wonders and how he was already believed by many to be a God, in that after death he had risen from the dead. . . . Tiberius referred the report to the Senate, which rejected it because it had not previously tested the matter, for *an ancient law prevailed* that no one should be held as a "God" by the Romans except by a vote and decree of the Senate. . . . The Romans rejected the report sent to it concerning [JESUS] . . . but Tiberius kept the opinion which he had formerly held and made no wicked plans against the teaching of Christ.

In the history book written by Eusebius (book 1: p. 111) Tiberius was Emperor during Jesus time and had bishops stationed all over the Roman Empire. Tiberius died two years after Jesus rose from the dead. He did not hear of Jesus until Pilate informed him. This shows that the Catholic religion was not Christian at that time and for a long time afterward. So it could not have been the Church that Jesus was building.

The Church that was being built on the Rock **[Jesus is the Christ]** was known by the name of *The Way*. The twelve Apostles were the teachers and leaders to those in this church, according to the command Jesus gave to them — "Feed My sheep!"

Apostle Peter explained to the Jews how to be saved — by believing in Jesus. To prove that Jesus was not dead many of the sick and lame were being healed in Jesus' name. This proved to the people that Jesus was alive and building His Church.

Catholicism was the religion of the city of Rome by which the government controlled the entire Roman Empire. So naturally, the Roman Empire religion had to possess

Jesus, The Way

everything that pertained to anything religious. That is why it claimed Peter as the first pope.

However, it was impossible for Peter to be the first pope because he would have had to be the metropolitan bishop of Rome before becoming a pope and besides the office of pope did not exist until sometime later when the Roman Empire broke up and there was no longer an emperor to be the pontifex maximus.

I don't think the Catholics were as interested in Peter as they were in his keys — the keys that Jesus said He was going to give him. Now all the popes display keys they claim have been handed down from Peter.

With these keys the pope is now presumably able to lock up Heaven and open wide the gates of Hell. Anyone who is **"excommunicated,"** that is forbidden the Catholic type of communion called the Eucharist — which the Catholics claim to be essential to salvation — **can go to hell!**

The pope of the eastern half of the Roman Empire had a quarrel with the pope of Rome about the worshiping of statues. He excommunicated the pope of Rome so that the pope was forbidden to have the Eucharist. The pope of Rome retaliated by excommunicating the Eastern pope — so now **both can go to hell!**

The Romans could not believe in the Hebrew's God because He was only one God. The Roman Catholic pagan religion worshiped all their gods in groups of three (Trinity). So the Catholics changed the Hebrew's God to be a Trinity — God the Father, God the Son and God the Holy Ghost.

This, however, is not according to the Old or New Testament. There is only one God mentioned; the Word of God and also the Spirit of Truth are of the One Invisible God!

It is a proven fact that Peter was not a pope and was never in Rome. Paul was in Rome for several years as a

Day Six

prisoner, while there he wrote several letters and in none of the letters did Paul mention Peter as being in Rome nor as a pope.

Another thing to consider is that Paul made an agreement with Peter that Peter should teach the Jews and Paul teach the Gentiles, so why should Peter go to Rome and be a pope of the Catholic pagans? Paul, in a letter to the Galatians, tells them about this agreement:

> But on the contrary, seeing that I had been entrusted with the gospel to the uncircumcised, just as Peter had been to the circumcised **(for He who effectually worked for Peter in his apostleship to the circumcised effectually worked for me also to the Gentiles)**, and recognizing the grace that had been given to me, James and Cephas [Peter] and John, who were reputed to be pillars, gave to me . . . the right hand of fellowship, that we might go to the Gentiles, and they to the circumcised.
>
> Galatians 2:7-9

I think we know enough about Jesus and His Church to start criticizing the theologians when they don't stick to the written word, and also the fundamentalists who stick to the word but don't understand it. We will first investigate the Roman Catholic church to see what's wrong. Why are they so different from the original Church that was called **The Way?**

Chapter 14

Lucifer and the Curse

LUCIFER

The name Lucifer (carrier of light) is not used much in the Hebrew Bible. For many thousand years the people did not know that light had to travel on something. They saw the Sun and assumed it took away the darkness so they could see, not knowing that the light had to travel from its source on something the scientists named **"ether."** The meaning of the name *Lucifer* is explained in the encyclopedia:

> LUCIFER, (1) in ancient astronomy, the morning star. A name given to the planet Venus when *she* appears in the morning before sunrise. When Venus follows the sun, or appears in the evening, *she* **is called Hesperus,** the evening star. (2) A name commonly given to **Satan,** *the prince of darkness,* . . . .

Another article in the same Encyclopedia that has a close connection:

> LUCINA, in Roman mythology, the **goddess of light** a surname of Juno (according to some **Diana;** according to others the name

Day Six

> of a daughter of Jupiter [Juno] derived from the root of lucco *[I shine]*). *Her* festival was celebrated 1 March, . . . in **her temple,** adorned with flowers . . . .

The articles just read indicate that Lucifer is a female. Let's search the Scriptures that are in the Hebrew Bible to see if Lucifer is really a female This account is written in the Bible:.

> Then all the men which knew that their wives had burned incense unto other gods, and all the women that stood by, a great multitude, even all the people that dwelt in the land of Egypt, answered Jeremiah, saying, As for the word that thou hast spoken unto us in the name of the Lord, we will not hearken unto thee. But we will certainly do whatsoever thing goeth forth out of our own mouth, to burn incense unto the **queen** of heaven, and to pour out drink offerings unto **her,** as we have done, we, and our fathers, our kings, and our princes, in the cities of Judah, **and in the streets of Jerusalem:** for then had we plenty of victuals, and were well and saw no evil. But since we left off to burn incense to the *queen of heaven,* and to pour out drink offerings unto **her,** we have wanted all things, and have been consumed by the sword and by the famine.
>
>   Jeremiah 44: 15-20

This indicates that Lucifer, better known as Queen of heaven, was deceiving the Jews into worshiping her by threats of violence. If they burned incense and poured out drink offerings to her, she left them alone. She did

Lucifer and the Curse

not bring famine to the Hebrews nor the sword.

One of the names most often used instead of the name *Lucifer* (light bearer) is *Satan*, which means adversary.

Another name given to Lucifer is *Devil* which indicates an evil spirit. Nevertheless all such names refer to Lucifer. This medium that conveys light (known as "ether") is not an inert substance, but is a great, powerful spirit, named *Lucifer*, who is God's enemy.

We have already read that Lucifer became proud because of her beauty, and thought she was equal with God. She had never tested her strength in a struggle with God, but had always obeyed.

In the Vatican there is a beautiful marble statue called the *Pieta*. The definition of the word *pieta*:

> pieta n. [It.; L. pietas, piety] a representation in painting, sculpture, etc. of Mary, the mother, grieving over the body of Jesus after the Crucifixion."

The encyclopedia gives just a little different account:

> PIETA, Italian term for representation, in painting or sculpture, of the **Virgin** mourning over the dead Christ taken down from the cross; . . . . The episode has formed the motive of innumerable pictures, . . . The Italian word *pieta* means piety, compassion.

I studied this beautiful sculpture, that is in the Vatican, very thoroughly because it did not seem just right. Mary, the Virgin, looked too young to be Jesus' mother. Suppose that Mary was only fourteen when she gave birth to her first child Jesus, and Jesus was thirty-three when he died. Then the age of Mary would be forty-

Day Six

seven years old — not a very young, beautiful lady, as in the pieta.

The mother, Mary, in the sculpture, was young with clean, well defined, smooth features; her head tilted a little to the right. She showed no remorse or sorrow or fondled the dead body of Jesus with love. In fact the dead body of Jesus was not well supported; the head hung far back. Mary's expression showed no love, only the look of triumph and victory in her whole being.

There was an art and novelty store close by that sold religious articles, charms and statues of gods by various names. Displayed in a prominent place was a statue of Diana. The virgin mother looked exactly like Diana. Her head was tilted to the right the same as Diana, and the features were identical. Mary, portrayed in the sculpture, and the goddess Diana are the same individual.

We do not have Jesus' mother at the foot of the cross, we have the goddess Diana in her pride — proud of her victory in nailing Jesus to the cross.

In paganism there is no Satan or Devil, all are gods or goddesses. The most highly worshiped are the goddesses, especially Diana and her Greek counterpart Artemis — which means Diana in Rome. The virgin was gifted with perpetual youth and beauty. Let's read what the Encyclopedia has to say about Diana:

> DIANA, a goddess of Italy whom the Romans subsequently identified with the Greek Artemis (q.v.). Diana was the protectress of slaves, who held a yearly festival in her honor. She was a virgin and no man was permitted to enter her temple. She dwelt in the **groves** and near wells. Madness and enthusiasm might be aroused in the hearts of men by this goddess. She was also the goddess of the moon, which fact accounts for her identification with the Greek moon-

goddess, Artemis. She seems to have been . . . the patron deity of the . . . Latins.
Encyclopedia Americana, book 9:68

Another account of her temple.

DIANA, temple of, a splendid structure and one of the glories of the ancient world, erected at Ephesus in Asia Minor. It was erected . . . in the year 620 B.C. and became a place of pilgrimage . . .. At the end [of] the temple was erected the golden statue of Diana.

Since ancient times man has believed in a virgin, female goddess. The priests usually built an elaborate shrine for the goddess so that the believing pagans could pilgrimage there to worship and donate part of their wealth — some have proven very profitable.

Although these virgin goddesses may have had different names, such as Diana, Artemis, Virgin, Queen of heaven, Our Lady and Madonna they all represent the same individual — Lucifer.

Probably the most ancient goddess that depicted Lucifer's beginning was named **"Nox."** She was born as a daughter of Chaos, (that is she was born at the time the Earth was just being formed and in total darkness).

It is said, "She gave birth to day and light." She is called mother of all things, of gods as well as men. A statue of her is in *Diana's temple at Ephesus*. Black sheep were sacrificed to her and also a cock was offered because the bird proclaimed the approach of day. She holds two children under her arms; one is black, representing night or death, the other is white denoting day.

Is there any similarity between these virgin goddesses and Lucifer? It seems illogical to compare Lucifer, who is referred to as "he" in the scripture, with a female goddess. But let's try.

Day Six

The English language is the only language that uses a neuter gender pronoun (it). So in translating old transcripts that use the word *he* instead of *it*, the translation is to *he* or *him*. Therefore we can't rely too strongly on the meaning of a personal pronoun — such as *he* or *she*.

The pronoun that we are concerned with, in this study, is *us*, which means two individuals at least. It also has the meaning of *we*.

God gives an abbreviated explanation about His work of creation up to the Sixth Day, and then He tells in detail about the creation of man. Let's examine this scripture leaving out all unnecessary remarks and descriptions so as not to be distracted:

> And God said, Let **us** make man in **our** image, after **our** likeness: . . . ***male and female*** . . . .
> Genesis 1:26

It's reasonable to believe that God was not talking to himself, but to someone else. Some say God was talking to Jesus the Christ, the word of God, but that could not be because the "Word" was part of God — he would be talking to himself. Neither could it be an angel because it is written that the angels are messengers, neither male nor female.

Lucifer is not an angel, as so many believe, she was created separately from the angels. She was created when God said, "Let there be light" for the purpose of carrying light from God to the Earth so that the Earth would not remain in darkness. Lucifer, as a light-bearer, was very essential to the working of God's plan of creation.

Now God is speaking to someone who is referred to as *us*. We know God is a male because God is known as Father. So let us suppose, *for now*, that Lucifer is a

Lucifer and the Curse

female. God said to Lucifer,

> Let us make man in our image, after our likeness — male and female.

After Eve was deceived and ate the forbidden fruit, the Lord God said to Lucifer:

> Behold, the man is become as one of us, to know good and evil: . . . .

This may be difficult for some to believe. Read it in the Bible — it is really there. Lucifer **is** a female.

PETER UNLOCKS THE PLAN TO SALVATION

We will now skip forwards a few thousand years to the time of the Church. Not the Roman Catholic Church but the Church called **The Way,** and see how Peter used the *so-called keys* to unlock the Scriptures, and to enlighten the Jews of the real working plan of salvation. The account will be abridged so that we will only get the bare facts.

> . . . and when the day of Pentecost was fully come, . . . *suddenly there came a* **sound** *from heaven* **as of a rushing mighty wind,** . . . And there *appeared* unto them cloven tongues *like as of fire,* and it sat upon each of them. And they were all filled with Holy Spirit.
> And there were **dwelling at Jerusalem** Jews . . .of every nation . . . now when this *sound like wind was heard* the multitude came . . . and were confounded, because that every man heard them speak in his own

Day Six

> language.... But Peter standing up with the eleven, [Apostles] ... said unto them, ... This is that which was spoken by the prophet Joel; And it shall come to pass in the last days, saith God, I will pour out my Spirit upon all flesh: ... and it shall come to pass, that *whosoever* shall call on *the name of the Lord* **shall be saved.** ... Therefore let all the house of Israel know assuredly, that God hath made that same Jesus, whom ye have crucified, both Lord and *Christ.* Now when they heard this ... [they said] ... **"What shall we do?"** Then Peter said ... "Repent, and be baptized every one of you in the *name of Jesus Christ for the remission of sins*, and ye shall receive the gift of the Holy Spirit."
> Acts, 2: 1-38

Peter at this time **unlocked** the Scripture revealing to the Jews that Jesus was the Christ **(the anointed)** and by Him *only* can they be saved.

These Jews that Peter is now talking to are the ones that stood before Pilate and demanded that Jesus be crucified. When Pilate reneged **the Jews put a curse on themselves by saying, let his blood be on our own head and on our children.** When these Jews heard that "only" by Jesus could they be saved. They exclaimed, "What shall *we* do!"

Peter replied, "Repent, and be baptized every one of you in the name of Jesus [the] Christ for the remission of sins, and ye shall receive the gift of the Holy Spirit."

When Peter made this statement he released the Jews from their **own curse.** This was the fulfillment of the promise Jesus gave to Peter when He said that what you release on earth will be released in heaven.

Satan is going to work like the devil to destroy this

Church known as "The Way." This Church is not a building; a State Religion or an organized denomination, but consists of all the people who believe that Jesus is the Christ. This group of people, known as the Church, is the spiritual body of Jesus The Anointed.

By whatever name is given to Lucifer she is going to fight by force and by deceit to try and destroy this body of people and set up a church of her own. ***This she has successfully done.***

Part IV

Catholic Church

Day Six

worship had to be dressed in white. Jupiter's priests also wore white hats, and only white animals were used in sacrificing to him. Elaborate shrines were built to worship Jupiter. Also an elite priestly organization was closely connected with the imperial government of Rome.

The Pontifex Maximus, who **was also the bishop of Rome,** had many bishops under him. These bishops were the head authority in every city all over the Roman Empire in order to rule the world by the pagan Roman Catholic religion The dictionary explains the meaning of pontifex:

> pontifex . . . in ancient Rome, a member of the supreme college of priests, the Pontifical College.
> pontiff . . . 1. a pontifex. 2. a bishop. 3. the Pope. 4. a high priest.

The encyclopedia gives us better information.

> PONTIFEX, one of the highest priestly colleges at Rome, *to which was entrusted the oversight of all religious observances, public or private.* Their institution, like that of all important matters of religion, was ascribed to Numa. The number of pontifices was originally probably six, all patricians, exclusive of the king, whose place, **after the abolition of the monarchy,** was taken by the pontifex maximus, or chief priest. The Ogulnian Law (300 B.C.) raised this number to eight, or, including the pontifex maximus, to nine, five of whom were to be plebeians. Sulla increased the number to 15 and Julius Caesar to 16, including in both these instances the pontifex maximus. The duty of the dignitary

Pagan Mass

was the inauguration of the priests, and in earlier times the care of the public records. He also superintended the sacred rites of Vesta, held his office for life, and could not leave Italy. The emperors afterward assumed this title until the time of Theodosius, and it was subsequently *assumed* by the **Christian bishop of Rome.** The pontifices also had the care of the calendar, and decided lawsuits which were connected with religion. The external badge of the pontifex, at least on solemn occasions and while engaged in the duties of his office, was **a dress bordered with** *purple, and a tapering hat* made of the [white] skins of sacrificed animals.

This was the Catholic Church in its infancy, 300 years before Jesus and to 300 years after the time of Jesus. Even at its earliest period it was known as Catholic. The bishops today try to tell us that the word *Catholic* means the church was every place in the world. That is not the truth Israel and Judah were not Catholic. Neither were the Arabs nor, at first, the countries of Europe. The word *Catholic* indicates that the Romans accept, and worshiped all the gods of the different nations of the entire world Except, of course, the only *one* God of the Hebrews. Later however the Catholics converted the God of the Hebrews into a Trinity (God the father. God the son, and God the holy ghost so that these three gods could be added to the rest of their many gods.

There is an interesting article named "Triumph" in the *New Americanized Encyclopedia*, Page 5925 copy:

> Triumph, an honor awarded to generals in ancient Rome for decisive victories over

Day Six

foreign enemies; . . . . The triumph consisted of a solemn procession, which, starting from the Campus Martius outside the city walls, passed through the city to the Capitol. Rome was en fete, the streets gay with garlands, the temples open. The procession was headed by the magistrates and senate, who were followed by trumpeters and then by the spoils, which included not only arms, standards, statues, etc., but also representations of battles, ... Next came the victims destined for sacrifice, especially white oxen with gilded horns. They were followed by the prisoners who had not been sold as slaves but kept to grace the triumph; they were put to death when the procession reached the Capitol. The chariot which carried the victorious general (triumphator) was crowned with a laurel and drawn by four horses. The general was attired like Capitoline Jupiter in robes of purple and gold borrowed from the treasury of the god; in his right hand he held a laurel branch, in his left an ivory scepter with an eagle at the point. Above his head the golden crown of Jupiter was held by a slave who reminded him in the midst of his glory that he was a mortal man. . . . On reaching the temple of Jupiter on the Capitol, the general placed the laurel branch . . . on the lap of the image of the god, and then offered the thank offerings. A feast of the magistrates and senate, and sometimes of the soldiers and people, concluded the ceremony.

This is how the pagan Romans lived. They worshiped

Pagan Mass

statues and many imaginary gods. The Romans were Catholic from their very beginning, up to the time of Constantine and from then on. The duty of the Emperor and his staff of bishops was to protect the Catholic belief from any heresy, even to the shedding of the heretic's blood.

The Catholic Church is the same today except for a few alterations to keep up with modern style. The Church still has solemn processions. The pope and bishops wear white dresses (like a goddess) and a white pointed hat However now the pope rides on an elevated chair carried by four men instead of a four-horse chariot. Instead of an ivory scepter he carries a cross with Jesus still nailed to it (called the crucifix). The Catholics have never taken Jesus down from the cross and they sacrifice him many hundreds of times daily in the **celebration of Mass.**

The Catholic Church has changed the meaning of the word *Mass* to mean one of their sacraments — the Eucharist or Communion. The dictionary gives us some of the changed meanings of the word.

> Mass . . . LL. messa, dismissal L. missa, . . . to dismiss . . .(go, you are dismissed), addressed to the congregation by the priest toward the end of the service. 1. the celebration or service of the Eucharist, a sacrament of the Roman Catholic Church, consisting of a series of prayers and *ceremonies*: **High Mass is *celebrated*** with *incense* and music, ...

There is going to be a great deal of misunderstanding in the use of this word *Mass* because the Catholics have changed the meaning so many times.

Originally the Catholic religion did not believe in the God of the Hebrews nor know any thing about Jesus.

Day Six

They spent their time in temples worshiping Greek gods, statues and the Emperor.

Several hundred years, after Jesus, some of the bishops in Asia and Africa may have read some letters or a Gospel written by Mark, or maybe some other apostle, about Jesus being crucified **(crucifying a Jew they liked very much)** and then they added this religion of Jesus being crucified to their pagan ceremonies.

The Romans were never satisfied with simple and natural actions of everyday life. Everything had to be performed by a bishop or priest; always with the same magic words and great ceremony, in order to charm their favorite gods into doing what they desired.

We will now read from the encyclopedia about Mass. This article is too long to copy in full so we will only pick out parts that we need. This treatise is a little bit biased — it was written by a Catholic professor.

Emphasis by J.A.

> The MASS. According to the **teaching** of the *Catholic* Church the Eucharist is the Sacrament which contains the body and blood, soul and divinity, of Jesus Christ under the appearance of bread and wine. At the Last Supper, the night before He died, Christ, . . . instituted the Eucharist by taking bread, giving thanks, blessing the bread, breaking it, and giving it to the apostles, saying, "Take ye and eat. This is my body." And the cup of wine . . . . "This is my blood which shall be shed for the remission of sins. Do this for a ***commemoration*** *of me.*"

The word *commemoration*, meaning to *celebrate*, is not in the Bible. The word used by Jesus is remembrance. The broken bread represented Jesus' body, badly bruised

Pagan Mass

and broken. The drinking of the wine represented the blood of Jesus. This simple act was for the remembrance of the sacrifice Jesus was about to undergo.

Still reading the Encyclopedia:

> The [Catholic] Church teaches that, when Christ said, "This is my body" the substance of the bread was, by His almighty power, **changed** into the substance of His body, and that, when He said, "This is my blood," the substance of the wine was similarly changed into the substance of His blood, while the **appearances of bread and wine remained.** *The Church further teaches* that the change of bread and wine into the body and blood of Christ, called Transubstantiation continues to be made by Jesus through the *ministry of His priests*, to whom through the apostles and their successors, He gave this miraculous power when He said, "Do this for a commemoration of me." The priests exercise this power of Transubstantiation through the words of consecration in the Mass. What, then, is the Mass? The Mass is the solemn memory, with a narrative, of Christ's passion and death. It is the *perpetual sacrifice of the New Covenant.*
>
> In the *catechism* it is described as the unbloody sacrifice of the body and blood of Christ. As in the offering of this sacrifice, **certain words** and actions in fixed form are used, the Mass may be defined as the aggregate of prayers and ceremonies which constitute the service of the Eucharist in the Latin, that is, the **Roman and Gallican, rites.**

Day Six

There is confusion in the meaning of words and actions in this explanation of the ceremony of "Mass." First of all, the Greek word *Christ* which means **anointed,** is not the name of anybody, and does not specify anyone in particular. King Saul was Christ (he was anointed), so were Kings David and Solomon. Do the Catholics refer to one of these men when they say Christ? Why don't they ever say Jesus the Christ, or Jesus the Anointed?

The article also stated, "the perpetual sacrifice of the new covenant." The sacrifice was not perpetual. It was performed only once. The sacrifice of Jesus was not the new covenant. Jesus completely fulfilled the Law, overcame the sins of this world and was sacrificed. His blood was poured out to cover the sins of man. He rose from the dead, thereby establishing a new covenant.

In the catechism, the Mass is described as the unbloody sacrifice of the body and blood of Christ. Didn't Jesus the Christ shed any blood when he was sacrificed? The scripture says that, "By his blood our sins are covered." Exact words and certain actions in fixed forms, by the bishop or priest, are used. This really is confusing. Are the bishops and priest trying to *charm* God into doing things for them that He would not otherwise do? Are the priests and bishops **wizards using magic to influence God?**

Let's read more from this article and see if we can find out what the word *mass* really means and why it was used:

> . . . liturgy, rite; still survives in the Eastern Church, and "holy liturgy" corresponds exactly to the word *Mass.* This latter term has become the recognized and almost exclusive technical name for the liturgy of the West. *Its derivation is even yet not quite certain*; but it is generally said to be a late

Pagan Mass

Latin verbal noun for *missio (dimissio)*, from the verb *mittere*, to send, send away.

Primarily, missa was used in the sense of "dismissal" with reference to the concluding part of the service, and then, *by a gradual process* .... The first time we know for certain that it was employed in its **present sense** was in the **4th century, about 385 or 386,** in a letter of Saint Ambrose to his sister, in which occurs the statement , ... (== I begin to say Mass). A 2d century instance of the use of the word *missa* in this sense is of doubtful authenticity. . . . So much for the word, which is clearly "much later" than what it denotes ....

In the *2d century* there is very probably an interesting allusion to the Mass from the outside, in a letter written by the pagan, Pliny the Younger ... governor of Bithynia, to the Emperor Trajan about 111-113. ...

— P.J.Lennox,
Professor of English Language and Literature,
The **Catholic** University of America.
Volume 18: pp. 393-399.

Is it possible that Saint Ambrose, **a bishop,** was just beginning to learn to celebrate Mass? Where was this word *Mass* used in his letter to his sister, at the beginning or end of the letter? If at the end of the letter it could mean "I must go." This would be similar to the way we end letters today by saying Good By, or Sincerely yours, or maybe, So long. My mother always ended her letters by saying May heaven protect you from your loving mother.

P.J.Lennox did not tell us what the pagan governor

Day Six

said in his letter It seems very difficult to find any thing for sure and complete about the Catholic Church! **Why is it so secret and guarded?**

Who had the authority to make Bishop Ambrose a saint? Only a pope has that power, and at this time of history there was no pope, only pagan bishops under a pagan emperor, the Pontifex Maximus. Ambrose must have been sainted many years later when there was a pope. And why was he sainted? He wrote a letter.

Lets search what the Roman pagan Catholics were doing at this time, that is, after Jesus was sacrificed and before Jerusalem was destroyed by the Roman Catholics.

The Romans were pagans and worshiped the emperor as a god along with their other gods and goddesses. Nero was an emperor and was worshiped as a god. The *Encyclopedia Americana* gives this account of Nero:

> . . . during his reign, in 64 a.d., a great conflagration took place at Rome, ... Nero was commonly suspected of being the originator of the fire . . . Nero did his utmost to transfer the guilt of this action to the Christians, whom he caused to be cruelly persecuted for it throughout the empire.

If Nero persecuted the Christians throughout the whole Roman Empire, he certainly was not able to do it all by himself — he needed lots of help. Because Nero was the Emperor, he was also the Pontifex maximus, (head bishop of Rome) with many bishops under his authority throughout the empire. These metropolitan bishops, and the lesser bishops under them, carried out Nero's orders. They did not automatically persecute everyone they thought to be Christian but gave each suspect a chance to prove himself. If the accused would pour out a libation or burn incense to the Emperor god Nero, that would prove he was a faithful Catholic. There was a small percentage taken who believed that Jesus was the Christ. These were killed.

Most of the so-called Christians at this time were pagans and only added belief in Jesus to their worship of their other gods, they poured out a libation and burned incense to Nero their god.

DIFFERENT RELIGIOUS BELIEFS

During the first hundred years A.D. some of the eastern metropolitan bishops got tired of worshiping so many gods, besides there was nothing to gain in this pagan religion except to keep peace with their gods. The Catholics had no hope of eternal life — only the fear of death.

In the book *World History* is found this recording of history.

> For *three* centuries the Christians suffered intermittent persecution. . . . remember that for long periods the Christians were permitted to worship as they wished without interference, that during long periods of freedom and relative security they won many converts among all classes and nationalities in the Empire. This is easy to understand when we recall that Christianity was but one of a number of *eastern religions* that were being taken up by the Romans and Greeks who had long since ceased to believe in the old gods. Outstanding among the cults widely current in the **third century** was that of the Cybele, the **Great Mother.** Others who were worshiped were: Attis; the Egyptian Isis and

Day Six

Serapis; the Babylonian goddess Ishtar; and Bel Atayatis. Most widely followed of all, and similar to Christianity in many of its teachings and practices, was the cult of Mithras, one of the Persian deities. Points of similarity between Mithraism and Christianity were to be found in their belief in heaven and hell, in the immortality of the soul and the last judgment, in their concept of the unceasing struggle between the forces of good and evil in the world. Both religions **sanctified** Sunday among the days of the week and as **a special feast the twenty-fifth of December.** In their ceremonies both made use of the bell, holy water, and candle. Mithraism reached the height of its popularity around 275 a.d. after which it underwent a decline. It is vary likely that because of the similarity of many of its teachings to those of Christianity it prepared the way for a wider acceptance of Christianity in the Empire . . . .

The last serious **persecution of the Christians** occurred under the Emperor Decius **(250-251).** Edicts of toleration, . . . were issued in 311 and 313 [sixty years later] by Galerius and Constantine. The Emperor Constantine recognized that while the Christians numbered scarcely a tenth of the population, they constituted the most potent spiritual force in the Empire. . . . Christian bishops were appointed to the posts in the Roman administration.

It is very apparent that the one who wrote this did not know the difference between Christian and Catholic beliefs. Christians believed in one God only and they did

Pagan Mass

not use any kind of Catholic ceremony or use bells and candles or have pagan practices such as using holy water. Maybe the author was reading from the catechism and thought it was the Bible.

Sunday is the first day of the week — not the last day. Supposing there were six days work to be done in seven days, would you rest on the first day or the last day? Constantine declared **Sun**day to be the day of rest. According to the **Roman calendar** Sunday was the first day of the week, named after the Sun. The theologians arrived at this conclusion because in the Hebrew Bible it states that Jesus, after He rose from the dead, visited the Apostles on the first day.

Now do a little thinking. The Hebrews day ended at sundown, not midnight as it did with the Romans. So on the sixth day ("Saturday") the Apostles worshiped their God in the temple, about three in the afternoon, and then went to their place of lodging. When Jesus visited them — it was still the sixth day. They rested on the seventh day and In the morning, the first day of the week, (Sunday) it was time to go to work.

Reading from the same book:

> By the fourth century, that is *three hundred years* after Jesus, in spite of popular misunderstanding, and **occasional persecution,** Christianity had become a legally recognized religion. Constantine now sought to strengthen the unity of the Empire and to buttress a government, which had already revealed many signs of weakness, by winning the allegiance of the Christians. . . .
>
> In time, ancient [pagan] temples were turned over to the Christians as places of worship, their property was exempted from taxation, they were permitted to hold and

Day Six

inherit property, and the emperor made rich gifts to Christian churches.

Really there were no such things as Christian Churches at this time. The real believers themselves were the church and they met in any building or open place wherever it was available.

The metropolitan bishops, from the eastern part of the Roman Empire, were the ones that formed this so called Christian Church. In so doing they were adding belief about Jesus to their pagan doctrine.

Constantine saw the strength in this group so he favored them but only to increase his own prestige. Constantine recognized the Christians numbered only a tenth of the population but understood they were the most powerful spiritual force in the Empire. Let's read and learn what this Christian organization believed:

**WORLD HISTORY
at a glance**

At the very moment when Constantine succeeded in strengthening the unity and administration of the Empire with the help of the Christians, there occurred a serious division in the ranks of the Christians themselves. The Greek speaking Eastern half of the Roman Empire had always exhibited a taste for philosophical and religious controversy. The very language lent itself to the refinement of distinction and the logical opposition of concepts.

There now arose a controversy revolving about the exact nature of the divinity of Jesus. The *long-accepted* view of God was

Pagan Mass

that he was "one" and indivisible but possessed of **three** divine persons: God the Father, God the Son who had come among men and died on the cross, and God the Holy Ghost. An Alexandrine preacher, Arius, insisted that Jesus was inferior in divinity to God the Father. His reasoning, in part, was that Jesus, unlike the Father, had been created and had therefore not existed from the beginning; that he could not have been truly man without at the same time being less god. The question had many aspects and its debate stirred up the most intense excitement. . . .

Arius was opposed by many churchmen, most prominent among whom was the **bishop** Athanasius who, at one stage in the controversy, had to flee to Rome for safety.

In 325 A.D. there assembled in Nicaea, a city in Asia Minor not far from Constantinople, a council called together from all Christendom **by the emperor** for the purpose of settling the controversy which had created a schism in the [Catholic] church. After **long debate** the bishops condemned the doctrine of Arius and affirmed the principles upheld by Athanasius. Arian books were burned and the preaching of Arian doctrines prohibited.

The Emperor Constantine was using his bishops to stop anything that was not agreeable to the Catholics. In the *Encyclopedia* (Book 7: pp. 554-56) is an article about Constantine which describes his character and religious belief Why he is always called Constantine the Great.

. . . Flavius Valerius Aurelius Constantinus,

Day Six

called the Great, Roman emperor . . . . He was the son of the Emperor Constantinus Chlorus, and after the death of his father was chosen emperor by the soldiery, in the year 306. Galerius was very unwilling to allow him the title of Augustus, and gave him that of Caesar only. Constantine, however, took possession of the countries which had been subject to his father, ... He then directed his arms against Maxentius, who had joined Maximian against him.

In the campaign in Italy he saw, it is said, a flaming cross in the heavens, beneath the sun, bearing the inscription, . . . (Under this sign thou shalt "conquer"). He accordingly caused a standard to be made in this form, which was called the labarum. Some days after this he vanquished the Maxentius . . . . He then entered the city in triumph . . . . He was declared by the Senate chief, Augustus, and pontifcx maximus. In the year 313, together with Licinius, he published the memorable edict of **toleration** in favor of the Christians. By this everyone was allowed to embrace the religion most agreeable to his own mode of thinking, and all the property was restored to the Christians that had been taken from them during the persecutions. They were also made eligible to public office. This edict marks the period of the *triumph of the cross* and the downfall of paganism.

Just think about this for a minute or two and you will understand that the Roman government was never Christian. The dates given show that for almost 300 years after Jesus it was still Catholic and persecuted anyone who

Pagan Mass

believed Jesus rose from the dead. If you believe that you can conquer by the cross, and still keep **Jesus nailed to the cross** — you are safe from persecution.

The Roman Empire was divided into the Eastern part which was ruled by Licinius and the Western by Constantine. Licinius married Constantine's daughter but still was not friendly — he persecuted the real Christians. The two emperors took up arms against each other and Licinius was defeated and put to death at Constantine's command. Now Constantine was Emperor and pontifex maximus of both the eastern and western Roman Empire.

Still reading in the *Encyclopedia* about the death of Constantine to see if he believed as a Christian, or if he died a pagan.

> Thus the latter [Constantine] became, in 325, the sole head of the eastern an Western Empires. His first and chief cares were the establishment of peace and order, and the propagation of **his religion.** Many beneficial decrees were proclaimed by him. Among these were those which abolished all the establishments of debauchery, ... To the Christians he gave permission . . . to erect churches, but to be remunerated for the cost of them from his domains. Amidst all the cares of government and the occupations of war he found leisure to assemble the Council of Arles, to put an end to the schism of the Donatists. The ecumenical council held at Nice, in Bithynia 325 a.d. was attended by him in person. . . . Toward the close of his life he *favored* the Arians, . . . and he even banished many **Roman Catholic** *bishops.* In the year 337 he fell ill in the neighborhood of Nicomedia, was baptized,

Day Six

The Catholic Church still offers this baptism to any Catholic when he is about to die, even those who are condemned to death for murder. The name used now for this sacrament is called the **extreme unction.** It guarantees you won't go to Hell. Instead you will go to purgatory and stay there until the pope makes you a saint.

Back to reading the book:

> Constantine, who held absolute power in a violent age, had sinned much; his hands were stained with blood, not least with that of his son Crispus, accused by the Empress Fausta of an attack on her virtue. Fausta herself was the next victim, charged with false accusation, but while the true facts of the case are lost, the executions in both cases were by Constantine's order. His approach to Christianity was gradual and idiosyncratic. In 312 he probably knew little theology and less about the history and organization of the Church. Years later . . . he was able to preach an Easter sermon . . . . . He was fond of referring to himself as the bishop of those outside the Church, ...

Constantine never was a Christian. He remained always a Roman Catholic While he was dying, the Catholic bishops that were under his authority gave him the extreme unction. As it has been written — they baptized him. It would be difficult to place a dying man under water, so the bishops must have sprinkled water on him with a few magic words.

More of the same history:

Pagan Mass

Constantine's conversion has fascinated historians and psychologists for centuries. Yet, all is still not clear. The difficulty is twofold. First, the world of ideas of the early fourth century is strange to us, and many of the key facts are unknown. Second, there is the problem of entering into the mind of this unusual man — unusual to his contemporaries as well as to us. Ill-educated but fond of the company of scholars; gentle and humane, yet never hesitating before a battle or an assassination; superstitious and otherworldly, yet a realistic administrator and a bold and decisive reformer — Constantine was a man of many parts.

Today we know more about the fourth century than scholars did a generation or so ago. And it may be that we have a deeper understanding of psychology in general and religious psychology in particular than they had.

One long-held view can be rejected out of hand. According to this theory, Constantine's conversion was entirely a matter of policy, carefully and cynically calculated, and designed to win for him the support of a numerous and important group in the society of the time. But the Christians were neither numerous nor important, and this was especially true in the **western half of the Empire**.

It is true that Christians were more numerous in some of the eastern provinces. But in 312 the eastern provinces were not Constantine's problem, and even there Christians were far from forming a majority. It is un-

Day Six

> likely that Christians — **however we define them** — formed ten per cent of the population of the Empire. As for their importance, there were upper-class Christians, of course; but the bulk of the Christian community seems to have belonged to what we call the lower middle class of cities and towns — traders, artisans, small landowners and petty "rentiers," whose influence on the course of affairs was negligible. *Nowhere were the country people Christian.* And the army, whose support was crucial for Constantine until the last of his rivals had been eliminated, was and long *remained solidly pagan.* If Constantine's conversion was a matter of calculation it was an ill-considered one, and with no real bearing on his success. . . . He wanted to find God, but not in any spirit of humility; he was a man fully conscious of his mission and of his ability to accomplish it, if only the power that ruled the universe would help him.
>
> — Robert Browning

This doesn't speak well for Constantine's motif, caricature, or his pagan religion. The unknown god that he believed ruled the universe could have been Lucifer, better known as Diana. The article just quoted states that the majority of the Christians — "however we define them" formed ten percent of the population of the Empire. What was the other ninety percent? They were pagan Catholics! At the time of Constantine the Catholics were getting tired of worshiping the same old gods and pouring out libations to the Emperor.

The Catholics liked the idea of Jesus being nailed to the cross because the Roman Catholics had a strong hatred for the Jews. They had Jesus nailed on the cross and they were going to keep him there.

As has already been mentioned, the word *Christ* is a Greek word which means anointed. The Romans hated the Jews, so in mockery they called all those who believed that Jesus was the anointed, Christ. The Roman Catholics did not state that this new religion believed in Jesus, but believed in the anointed. So in ridicule they were called anointed. In the Greek language they were called Christ or Christians.

At first the Roman Bishops used the word *Christian* as a mockery for those who believed that Jesus was the Christ. Later the word gained favor and the Roman pagan Bishops appropriated the name Christian for their own religion. The eastern Bishops added the man Jesus, who had become known as a God, to their many other gods.

It is quite evident that Lucifer was working hard to upgrade her religion over that established by Jesus — which was called The Way. This expression came from the statement Jesus made when he said, "I am the way." I don't believe any denominational church today uses this name.

Lucifer taught, through Emperor Constantine, that an individual can conquer through the cross. Most so-called Christians wear a cross of some kind, thinking it is something holy. If your son was electrocuted for a crime, would you wear an electric chair symbol around your neck as a holy charm? This is some of Lucifer's deceitful, clever work!

Chapter 16

Catholic Cross

Studying world history we find that the Romans controlled the nations of the world by believing in and worshiping all known gods. The only exception was the God of the Hebrews.

The Romans believed in **the gods of all the nations that were under Roman control, and proudly called themselves *Catholic*.** By this acceptance and belief in all the known gods, the Romans ruled the entire Roman Empire. The Romans ruled by church laws, dogma, coercion and **corruption**. About three hundred years **after Jesus,** the Catholic bishops in the eastern part of the Empire were delving into new religious thoughts, such as "Mithraism," which had a *phony resemblance to Christianity*. In the *Encyclopedia* there is a description of this religion:

> MITHRAS, a Perso-Iranic divinity, first the god of the heavenly light and the lord of all countries, afterward the **sun,** or the genius of the sun, which was **worshiped as a deity** by the Persians and at a later period also in **Rome.**

In India there is another religion that is very similar to that found in Persia and known by almost the same name. It reads in part:.

> MITRA . . . (Sanskrit, meaning friend), an Indian god of light, belonging to the Vedic period. Mitra is the Friend, the personification of Daylight, a bright being . . . Mitra is identical with the Iranian Mithra, or Mithras, also a solar Deity and the central figure of a special cult.
> *Encyclopedia 19:271*

When Constantine was Emperor and Pontifex Maximus of the Roman Empire, there was a priest of the pagan Catholic religion named Arius, who tried to introduces a new belief into the firm doctrine of the Catholic church? The *Encyclopedia* gives this account of him:.

> ARIUS, a well-known name in ecclesiastical history, identified with the origin and **spread of the *first* great "heresy"** in the . . . [Catholic] Church. . . . He first comes clearly into view as a presbyter [priest] of the Church of Alexandria, in the commencement of the **4th century**, engaged in conflict with his bishop, Alexander. At a previous period he is said to have been connected with Meletian schism, and on this account to have been *excommunicated* by Peter of Alexandria, who had ordained him deacon.
> The views of Arius first attracted attention about, **310 A.D.** . . . Bishop Alexander, in addressing [teaching] the presbyters and other clergy on the doctrine of the **"Trinity"** dwelt so strongly on the consubstantial unity of the Father and the Son that Arius charged him with holding Sabellianism.
> Arius' belief is set forth in the following: "We believe," he says in the letter to Alexander,

Day Six

"in one God alone without birth, alone everlasting. . . . We believe that this God gave birth to the only begotten Son before eternal, through whom He made these periods and all things; *that he gave birth to Him*, not in semblance, but in truth giving Him a real existence, at His own will so as to be unchangeable, God's perfect creature, but not as other creatures. . . . not, as Valentins maintained, a development; nor as Sabellius, Son and Father at once, which is to make two out of one, . . . but created by the will of God, and endowed with His own glorious perfections — yet not so that the Father did thereby deprive himself of attributes which are his without origination, being the Source of all things; so that while there are *three persons* yet God is alone the Cause of all things and unoriginated.

"The Son on the other hand, is originate, begotten by the Father time-apart. The Son is not, therefore, co-eternal or co-unbegotten with the Father, as if these were two unbegotten principles; but God is before all things as single and the principle of all, and therefore, before Christ also."

Such were the questions which distracted the [Catholic] church beyond all precedent in the beginning of the **4th century,** and led to the "first" great ecumenical council, which was convened in Nicae in 325.

It requires only to be mentioned here, that *after various turns in the controversy*, it was **finally decided** against Arius, that the **Son** was "of the **same substance**" with the Father, "very God of very God." Although

Catholic Cross

defeated at the council of Nicae, Arius was by no means subdued. He obtained means of access of Constantia, the sister of the emperor, who, on her death-bed, strongly urged her brother to reconsider the question, and to recall the hersiarch from banishment.

Restored to court, he, [Arius] along with the Eusebian party, who, although professing to accept the Nicene doctrine, were in reality indifferent, if not hostile, to it, renewed the theological strife, in which Athanasius was nothing loath to join.

Interchanges, now of friendly recognition and now of menace passed betwixt the emperor and the intrepid bishop of Alexandria, who obstinately refused to reinstate Arius as presbyter. At length, on the banishment of Athanasius to Treves in 336, Arius returned to claim his old position; but even in the absence of the **bishop** the people rose in uproar against the heretic, and the emperor was forced to recall [Arius] to Constantinople.

There the bishop was reluctantly compelled to profess his willingness to receive him once more into the bosom of the [Catholic] Church, but before the act of admission was completed Arius was taken suddenly ill, while walking with a friend in the evening, and died in a few moments.

This account we just read shows that the Roman Empire, under the rule of Constantine was still pagan. The Catholics were quarreling over their new god they learned from the Jews. This episode took action some three hundred years after the four Gospels were written

Day Six

and all of Paul's letters and the Book of Revelations were available in writing. The Catholics refused to accept the teaching of the Apostles, that was on record, but were using their mythology to deny that the word of God became flesh. God did not give birth to Jesus — a woman gave birth to him. Therefore Jesus was the son of man. His body of flesh was not God but was the temple of God.

This present-day author, telling us about the pagan events of Constantine uses the name "Christian Church" which is not correct and misleading. The pagans were not Christian — they were Catholic! The Catholics were cleverly copying and mixing up the New Testament which was introduced to the Jews over three hundred years earlier.

Now the pagans are having a hard time deciding whether to accept Mitherism or Arian's mythology. Constantine favors Arian. Finally Constantine called his pagan, metropolitan bishops together, some from the eastern part of the Empire and some from the west and held a council at Niesa 312 A.D.

Arius, the priest, had already been excommunicated and now he is banished from the country. But later recalled by Constantine and given his old job back as priest. But before the bishop in Constantinople could complete the ceremony of reinstating him into the fold of the Catholics, he died suddenly while walking with a Catholic friend. Who needs an enemy when you have such good friends?

Constantine was a pagan and his whole army was also pagan. The question is: Why did he have all his soldiers paint a cross on their shields just before going to battle to subdue Maxentius — the Emperor?

The cross was not a religious symbol as we are led to believe. It was a symbol of Roman torture. Only the criminals and the enemy were subject to this kind of death. The soldiers of Maxentius, and Maxentius him-

Catholic Cross

self, were stricken with fear and terror when they saw the threat of being nailed to the cross and dying a slow, agonizing death. They all turned and ran across the bridge except Maxentius — he jumped into the river and drowned. Constantine won the battle, by the sign of the cross, instilling a deadly fear in the opposing troops.

He entered Rome without a battle and was declared, by the Senate, Pontifex Maximus. Constantine then became known as the Great. Constantine, the pontifex maximus, then ruled the Roman Empire through his Archbishops of the large cities who were the ruling force of the Empire.

THE EVOLUTION OF THE CROSS

In the *Encyclopedia* there is a description of the Roman Cross and how it gradually changed its use to fit the changing doctrine of the Catholic Church. Just a few remarks will be given so that you will be able to understand the present day use of the cross by the Catholics.

> The cross as a symbol dates back to an *unknown antiquity*. It was recognized in all countries throughout the world at all times. Before the present era the Buddhists, Brahmans and the Druids utilized the device. The Druids considered that the long arm of the cross symbolized the way of life, the short arms the three conditions of the spirit world equivalent to heaven, **purgatory** and hell.
> The principal forms of crosses used in the Catholic Church are . . . [the] Crux immissa . . . or Latin cross. . . . In the Constantinople council (680) the bleeding

Day Six

Lamb, heretofore figuring on the symbolic crucifix, was forbidden and the dying Savior's image on the cross was ordered to take its place, thus originating the present form of the crucifix to be displayed to the public.

RELIQUARY CROSSES

In the very early days of the Church, already, **relics** *of the saints* were being **enshrined.** The different churches emulated one another in obtaining relics of greater distinction than others, and in "enshrining" them in reliquaries each more elaborate and rich in gems and workmanship than the others. Nothing was more natural than that the **altar cross should itself become a container of Holy Relics.** . . . In the Middle Ages, *on certain religious processions,* the altar cross was carried in advance of the clergy and, at some fixed places called stations, the procession stopped. The cross was then lowered to receive the devout kisses of the populace. . . . Lastly, these crosses received the image of the crucified Savior. . . . A general feeling of repugnance toward the instrument of punishment which, among the Romans, was reserved only for the most infamous class of criminals, would for a long time prevent the early Christians from representing Christ upon the cross, and this feeling would have to be *conquered* before the crucifix could come into use in *public worship* . . . . Crucifixes appear to have been first used in public worship to-

Catholic Cross

ward the end of the **6th century** . . . and it was not till after the Trullan Council, held at Constantinople in **692,** which ordained that historic paintings should be preferred to emblems or symbolical figures, that the images of Christ crucified began to multiply.
Encyclopedia Volume 8: pp. 238-240

Notice that the pagan Catholics gradually changed the use of the plain cross to that of the Crucifix. The last date given was almost seven hundred years after the time of Jesus.

Lucifer is teaching the faithful Catholics to worship the cross Jesus was sacrificed on. She is using the *Fathers of her church* to do the teaching. The pope, the bishops and the priests, all who are called Fathers, do the teaching.

Moses had the same problem with the Hebrews when they were in the wilderness. The Hebrews came to a place were there were deadly, poisonous snakes that killed many. Moses fashioned a copper snake and nailed to it as a pole, so that those who were bitten by the snakes, if they looked at the symbol and believed they did not die.

Later the Hebrews started to worship the symbol, to the extent that Moses had to grind the whole thing into dust to stop such a pagan worship.

THE END OF THE ROMAN EMPIRE

When the Roman Empire was overrun by several savage tribes from the Far East, and also broken up into its many individual nations, there no longer was an Emperor to be the Pontifex Maximus. The old Roman Empire was broken up into its various nations and new European nations came into existence. The metropolitan

Day Six

bishop of Rome then assumed the title of Pontifex Maximus, who is now also known as the pope.

History records a long struggle by each succeeding pope to become the spiritual head of all the kings of Europe. One by one the pope induces the kings, of newly formed nations, to become Catholic — for their survival. Then each converted king makes a law that all his subjects had to be Catholic — or else.

Now we have the beginning of the *Christian* Catholic Church, but still Catholic in its belief. The only difference now is the names have been changed. Heroes are now called Saints; Virgin Diana is now known by the name of Virgin Mary, who is also known by the name of Madonna, Madam, Mother, Queen of Heaven and lately she has been given the title of Queen of the Earth.

In the Catholic Church are dozens of different Orders, such as, Nuns, Monks, priests, Fathers and Holy Offices. Also there are the popes, who claim to have the two Keys they received from the Apostle Simon Peter.

The Catholic Church is divided now, the Greek "orthodox" Church in Constantinople and the Roman Catholics in the west. As mentioned earlier, the Romans chose to keep the name Catholic. They are now copying the Christian religion instead of copying the Greek gods. As they did before, all names are being changed.

The Catholic Church is so protected from the public's eye that it would be impossible to do more than to give but a meager exposure of the Churches' secrets. We will now read some history taken from:

WORLD HISTORY
at a glance

Rome, like other feudal towns, was dominated by the Roman nobles. . . . from 896 to

Catholic Cross

963 there were twenty popes many of whom were murdered or deposed.

For a time Theophylactus and his notorious wife Theodora controlled the papacy. Their daughter Marozia, **mistress** of one pope, was the **mother** of another, John XI, whose son in turn became Pope John XII .p.154

... The period during the *tenth century* when the papal office was in control of the most disreputable of the "gangster politicians" of Rome is sometimes called the era of "pornography," the rule of the harlots. p.156

Otto [from Germany] summoned a council of the church to reform the conditions which he found in Rome. John XII was tried and deposed for "murder, sacrilege, and immorality."

Pope John XII got his ass kicked out of his own Vatican whore house. If Pope John XII managed to get the extreme unction, at the time of his death, he would have had a guarantee to go straight to Heaven. He was entitled to extreme unction because he had not been excommunicated — he was not locked out of heaven by the next pope. I wonder how long this corruption in the papacy continued. Maybe it never ended!

The Catholic Church is not subject to the civil criminal laws. The Church has a court all its own to protect the priests, bishops and popes. Once in a while there is a news item stating that some priest, or higher-up, committed a sex crime or is a homosexual — then that ends the news report. Usually the guilty priest or bishop is transferred to another diocese and there continues his sex crimes, careful not to get caught again.

Chapter 17

Catholic

We should know more about the teaching and belief practiced by the Catholic Church. The inner workings are held so secret that the best that can be done is to read what the Catholic Church is willing to tell us. There are many pamphlets put out by bishops explaining how to pray the Rosary, why we worship the Virgin and on many other subjects.

Here are a few pamphlets, (published *for Catholics* to read), that will give us a meager insight of the working and teaching of the Catholic Church:

WHY CATHOLICS PRAY TO THE BLESSED VIRGIN MARY:

Many *non*-Catholics have been trained from childhood to believe that one of the clear proofs of the falsity of Catholicism is to be found in the honor that is paid to the Blessed Virgin Mary in the Catholic Church, and in the **innumerable trusting prayers** that are offered to her by Catholics. At the same time it is true that many non-Catholics, when they learn what are the genuine foundations of Catholic devotion to Mary, are drawn by it so irresistible that ultimately they become Catholics. For the truth is very simple and clear, and is all contained in the following two truths:

1. **Mary is the *Mother* of God.** *Catholics* do not believe that God was bound by any compulsion to have a mother; they believe that He chose to have a Mother and all that this implies. He chose to permit His human body to be formed in her womb. He chose to permit her to bring Him forth as a tiny baby into the world. He chose to let her feed Him at her breast, carry Him in her arms, guard Him from danger, and teach Him as any child would be taught, to walk and speak and pray. He thereby chose to grant Mary a power over Him that only love can bestow. *Catholics believe* that in choosing a mother, **the Son of God** chose to grant her the power over His will that the love of a good mother always wields over a good son.

2. **Mary is a mother to *all men*.** **Catholics believe** that the Son of God chose to come into the world through a mother in order that that mother might accept as His brothers all the children of the sinful race of man. He set an example as to how she should be honored and loved. He prepared her for this motherhood of all by *asking her* to suffer every conceivable form of pain, thus teaching her sympathy for the sorrows of her children. Had she been His mother alone, He would have spared her from pain, because He had the power to do so and because He loved her with an infinite love.

Day Six

He wrought His first public miracle at her request, and when he was dying He reminded her that she had been destined from the beginning to be a Mother of all. **Catholics** therefore believe that Mary will be as eager to help them, in troubles of soul and body, as every natural mother is eager to promote the welfare of her child.

The rosaries that Catholics *recite* are but the expression of their belief in these two truths. They know that if *Mary speaks* to her divine Son in their behalf, there can be no doubt about their receiving an answer to their prayers.

Reprinted from **The Liquorian, a Catholic monthly magazine** published with ecclesiastical approval. Legion of Mary . . . .

If Mary is the "mother of God" and also the "mother of all men," (which includes me), then ***I am a half-brother of God.***

If Jesus were God, and his mother taught him to pray, **who did he pray to?** Surely not to himself but to **God — his father.**

Pope Pius XII authors a *Marian Year Prayer* to be recited by the faithful Catholics as they have been instructed. This is the prayer they can recite to get time off from Purgatory.

ENRAPTURED by the splendor of your Heavenly beauty / and impelled by the anxieties of the world / we cast ourselves into your arms, O, Immaculate Mother of Jesus / and our Mother, Mary, / confident of finding in your most loving heart / appeasement of our ardent desires, / and a safe harbor from the tempest / which beset us on every side.

Though degraded by our faults / and overwhelmed by infinite misery, / we admire and praise the peerless richness / of sublime gifts / with which God has filled you, / above every other mere creature, / from the first moment of your Conception / until the day on which, / **after your Assumption into Heaven,** / *He crowned you Queen of the Universe.*

O crystal fountain of Faith, / bathe our minds with the eternal truths! / O fragrant lily of all holiness, / captivate our hearts with your Heavenly perfume! / O conqueress of evil and death, / inspire in us a deep horror of sin / which makes the soul detestable to God / and a slave to hell!

O well-beloved of God, / hear the ardent cry which rises up from every heart / *in this year dedicated to you.* / Bend tenderly over our aching wounds. / Convert the wicked, / dry the tears of the afflicted and oppressed, / comfort the poor and humble, / quench hatreds, / sweeten harshness, / safeguard the flower of purity in youth, / protect the *holy Church,* / make all men feel the attraction of Christian goodness.

In your name, resounding harmoniously in Heaven, / may they recognize that they are brothers / and that the nations are members of one family / upon which may there shine forth / the sun of a universal and sincere peace.

Receive, O most sweet Mother, / our humble supplications / and above all obtain

Day Six

for us / that, one day, **happy with you,** / we may repeat *before your throne* / that hymn which today is sung on earth around **your altars.** / *You are all beautiful,* O Mary! / You are the glory, / you are the joy, / you are the honor of our people / Amen.

— **Pope Pius XII**
(official English translation)
Partial indulgence of 5 years every time the prayer is recited devoutly with a contrite heart. . . . reciting the prayer on the Feast of the Immaculate Conception 1953 and 1954 and every Saturday of the Marian Year.

THE PAULIST PRESS.

How lucky are the faithful Catholics that some pope declared a Marian Year so that they can escape a few thousand years from the tormenting flames of purgatory. Here is a one-leaf flier that does not make sense:

The Promises of Our Lord to St. Margaret Mary for Souls Devoted to His Heart

1. I will give them all the graces necessary in their state of life.
2. I will establish peace in their homes.
3. I will comfort them in all their afflictions.
4. I will be their secure refuge during life, and above all in death.
5. I will bestow abundant blessings upon all their undertakings.
6. Sinners shall find in my Heart the source and the infinite ocean of mercy.

7. Tepid souls shall become fervent.

8. Fervent souls shall quickly mount to high perfection.

9. I will bless every place in which an *image* of my Heart shall be exposed and honored.

10. I will give to priests the gift of touching the most hardened hearts.

11. Those who shall **promote this devotion** shall have their names written in my Heart, never to be effaced.

12. I promise thee in the excessive mercy of my Heart that my all-powerful love will grant to all those who communicate on the First Friday in nine consecutive months the grace of final penitence; they shall not die in my disgrace nor without receiving their Sacraments. My Divine Heart shall be their safe refuge in this last moment.

Imprimatur, N.Y., 1949. *Francis Cardinal Spellman*, apostles of prayer

I wonder what Lord made all these promises, especially number 9. It must have been some pagan god the Catholics believe in.

Here is another tract that tries to justify the fact Catholics believe in purgatory:

Did the Catholic Church *invent* PURGATORY?

Objection: One of the proofs of the falseness of the Catholic Church is its **invention** of the doctrine of Purgatory. Nowhere in the Bible can the word *Purgatory* be found. Moreover,

Day Six

the Bible tells us that if we believe in Christ we are saved, and that means we go to heaven or hell when we die, not to a fictitious Purgatory. It seems to be true, therefore, that "Purgatory" was invented by priests as a means of getting money from people on the plea that the priests would then get their friends out of Purgatory.

Answer: To deny the fact of Purgatory because the word itself is not found in the Bible is surely unreasonable. The question is, does the Bible ever speak as if there would be some atonement for sin after death, outside of the eternal punishment of hell? The answer is yes. Our Lord Himself spoke of one sin (the sin of speaking against the Holy Ghost) that "shall not be forgiven him in this world, nor in the world to come." He thereby clearly assumed that His hearers knew there was a process of atonement for some sins in the world to come. The place where that process is carried out is what Catholics call "Purgatory."

Reprinted from *The Liquorian*,
a Catholic monthly magazine

If the Catholics *named it "Purgatory"* they must have *invented* it.

Here is another pamphlet, (for Catholics to read), of 22 pages — too long to copy in full. It is to help Catholics who are praying to the Virgin Mary, so they can address her properly.

By Florent E. Franke, M.D.
FOREWORD:

These beautiful expressions of devotion

to the Mother of God have been taken from the two editions of the Raccolta listed below. The Raccolta is an official list of indulgenced prayers and practices and carries the approval of the Church. It is not implied that the expressions listed carry an *indulgence,* since in nearly all cases they constitute but a fraction of the indulgenced prayer. They are collected in a pamphlet so that in this age of Mary her children may more readily address her with a variety of terms of affection and endearment, recalling her great prerogatives and **her role in the divine plan of creation.**

Imprimatur; Joseph E. Ritter

INTRODUCTION

We read in the Bible that after the fall of Adam the Lord said to the serpent in Paradise, "I will put enmities between thee and the woman and thy seed and her seed and **she** shall crush thy head and thou shalt lie in wait for her heel." This is the warfare between **Lucifer and his followers** and **Mary and her followers.** The battle lines are being more sharply drawn every day. Communism is forcing a showdown. . . . **When you were baptized,** you directly or through your sponsors renounced Satan and all his works. This placed you on Mary's side, *the winning side,* Since God guaranteed her the victory. . . .

The titles which the Church bestows on her recall to our minds the variety and splendor of her attributes and the unique

Day Six

position she holds in the divine plan of creation. Let us consider a few to illustrate:

... Beloved **spouse** of the Spirit of God ... Joy of the universal Church ... Mother of God the son ... Channel whereby we receive all graces *needful for our salvation.* .. Ever sinless virgin ... **lady and mistress of the universe** ... our lady of ransom .. . Mary, virgin priest ... Mary virgin, **sun** without stain.

The great mediatrix between man and God ... **Enthroned** *above* **the starry sky** ... Holiest of all creatures of God ... *The salvation of the world* ... Mother queen of the holy rosary of Pompeii ...Mother of the eternal Word made flesh ... Queen and mother in the ancient land of Pompeii, **once the home of paganism** ... August and *living temple* of the most adorable **Trinity.**

This is but a scant sample. The whole list contains more than 700 titles. I wonder what the queen, Virgin Mother of God, is doing in the pagan city of Pompeii. I have a picture that was published in *The Southern Cross,* a Catholic paper. It shows and explains about Pope Pius XII kneeling and praying to the picture of the Virgin of Pompeii.

THE HOLY FATHER PRAYS

His Holiness Pope Pius XII kneels in his private chapel to offer a special prayer to the *famous Madonna di Pompeii* during the **observance of her feast day.**

Catholic

This picture sure raises lots of questions. Why does the pope have a private altar right there in the Vatican where there are many altars?

Why do Christian Churches use altars?

Does the pagan city, "Pompeii," have anything to do with Christianity and salvation? Who is this famous Madonna di Pompeii?

Could she be Lucifer in disguise?

Here is another pamphlet:

Why Catholics do not take part in Protestant services.

Question: Is it not intolerant on the part of the Catholic Church to *forbid its own people* to attend services in a Protestant Church, . . .?

Answer: That is because the principles underlying the Catholic religion and those that Protestants uphold are entirely different. **The Catholic Church rests on the principles that there can be *only one* true religion;** . . . [a Catholic] may not act as if it were not the **one true religion** . . . . It is not merely **a *law* of the Catholic Church that Catholics may not attend Protestant services;**

The Protestant church rests on the principles that every man has a right to use his own private judgment in matters of religion; . . . at the same time it would be contrary to Catholics' principles and conscience to attend any but Catholic services.

Reprinted from *The Liguorian*, **published with ecclesiastical approval.**

Day Six

contemplative orders. Perhaps the best known of the women's orders is the Carmelites, founded in **1492.** This had a somewhat mitigated rule, compared to the male Carmelites. But St. Teresa reformed the order with a strict observance of the rule in 1562.

Another well-known order is the Poor Clares, which is the second order founded by St. Francis of Assisi and St. Clare in 1212. There are several contemplative orders of *men* as well. Most of the orders and congregations founded centuries ago were contemplative. When the **great bishop, St. Francis de Sales,** founded the *Visitation Sisters*, he suffered *severe criticism.* . . . St. Bernard called contemplation the highest form of **human worship.** It consists in adoration of God and *complete self-surrender.* . . . The true contemplative nun separates herself as completely as possible from the world, at least in ONE sense. They live in a cloister, or enclosure, which cuts them off from *almost* all other persons not living within their religious community.

I *[the bishop]* recall once visiting a Carmelite convent before it was occupied by the Sisters. The refractory, the room in which meals are eaten, was furnished most sparingly. Tables were bare, benches replaced chairs and on the table of the Superior was **a human skull.** In each cell, the room in which the Sisters slept, had a **"cross,"** *not a crucifix.* It was explained to me that this meant the Sister was the *victim for this cross.*

This very ascetic life is difficult for most

of us to understand, perhaps more difficult for many Americans who live in relative comfort. In a worldly sense, it is nonsense. In a spiritual sense, it is magnificent. Try to view it through your spiritual lenses . . . . This is not the only way to salvation. . . .

When you visit your relative who is a contemplative nun next time, don't be annoyed by those bars. These are not really separating you from her or her from you . .
. . They are not barriers at all.

If the double row of bars are not barriers why do they have them? With the double row of bars between you and the nun, who is maybe your daughter or sister, she cannot slip you a note crying for help. If she asks for help to escape she will be heard by those who are listening to every word. The skull on the table and the cross in her room tells her what will be her fate — her doom.

The bishop who wrote this article, knew too much about the nun's living quarters to have gotten all this accurate detail before the place was occupied by the captive nuns.

The religion of the Catholic Church sure is different from that of the church called The Way.

Chapter 18

The Cross and The Inquisition

The Apostles of Jesus the Christ preached the gospel of the Kingdom of God *to the Jews*, many of whom were from all parts of the World, so that the knowledge of Jesus and his message was well-known every place. All the people in the whole Roman Empire had a chance to hear and know about Jesus. But the Catholic pagans remained pagan.

About three hundred years after the Roman government crucified Jesus, to satisfy the unbelieving Jews, Constantine decided to add a similar doctrine to the Roman religion. This similar religion was to conquer with the cross. The trend that brought this about, the bishops in the *eastern part* of the Empire were accepting different religious creeds of heretic versions that resembled Christianity. The Catholic bishops in the West began to persecute those who believed these heretic doctrines. The bishops in the East retaliated by burning the Catholic, pagan shrines and tearing down the altars to their gods.

Constantine, inspired by some force, called the eastern and western bishops together and held a conference in order to save the Roman Catholic religion and the Roman Empire. Constantine permitted the new creeds to exist. In fact helped them but ordered that they must remain Catholic. Now we have the nucleus on which the Catholics built the Catholic Church. The Catholic Church

The Cross and The Inquisition

today proclaims Constantine a saint, and fixes the 20th of May as his festival.

The Roman Empire gradually disintegrated to where there was no longer an Emperor to be the pontifex maximus. In order to keep the Catholic Church from also disintegrating, the metropolitan bishop of Rome claimed to be the pontifex maximus. This metropolitan bishop all ready had the title of "Papa," which means *father* — he now has the added title of pope.

History has revealed to us that many of the popes and the clergy of the Catholic Church were very evil — in fact scandalous and vicious. They were not only sexually immoral but politically corrupt.

As the centuries passed, the popes came and went, each working for his own pleasure and personal gain. The Catholic Church continued to dominate the world — forcing the kings to obey the edicts and dogmas of the Catholic doctrine. All the nations of Europe were dominated by Rome.

The *Encyclopedia Americana* states that: in 1510, Leo X issued a bull, granting an *indulgence* to all who should contribute to the rebuilding of Saint Peter's Church at Rome. A Dominican friar was named commissary of the indulgence for Saxony and the North of Germany. Martin Luther, **a Catholic priest,** did not like this scheme of the pope to raise money by granting lengthy indulgence — that is, time off from Purgatory. Martin Luther, the Catholic priest, made up a list of 95 theses against the pope and his doctrine. He nailed them to the Catholic Church door.

Luther remained a Catholic all his life, though years later he did give up being a priest and married a nun. At no time did he intend to reform the doctrine of the Catholic Church nor did he deny the supremacy of the chair of Saint Peter. Luther's actions were strictly political. Many of the German nobles encouraged him and

Day Six

protected him with their armed knights — they wanted to be relieved from continually paying fees to the pope for his religious service.

It was other leaders that urged the Reformation. Actually this Reformation was promoted by the Catholics in Europe, in an attempt to correct the evil and filth in the Church at Rome. There is a fairly good account of the Reformation in the *Encyclopedia:*.

THE REFORMATION

The Reformation was the movement in the religious life of western Europe in the **16th century** which resulted in the formation of the Protestant Church. At earlier periods there had been a feeling that conditions in the leadership of Christendom needed improvement and attempts at betterment were made along two distinct lines. The first was through the efforts of individual men, *monastic orders and general councils* to bring about changes for the better **within the Church** . . . . The papal chair had been occupied for half of a century by men who were not interested in the revival of **learning** and were more interested in Italian politics than they were in giving Christendom the kind of leadership which it needed. *Some of the popes were indifferent to religion and of immoral lives*. The reformation of the 16th century started as an effort to bring about *reforms within* the Roman Catholic Church, and it was only after this seemed *impossible* that the leaders *withdrew from organized Roman Catholicism.*

The Cross and The Inquisition

There are a number of reasons why the separation from the Church and the formation of a new organization met with success in the 16th century when the earlier efforts had failed. Most important of all was the *revival* of learning. Men were thinking for themselves as they had not before *for centuries*. The invention of printing brought about wide diffusion of knowledge. There was an opportunity through the study of writings of the Early Church fathers to compare the Church of the first centuries in its belief and organization with the Church of the 16th century. It was evident to students that there was a wide difference between the two. The circulation of the New Testament also tended to bring about a diversity of opinion on religious matters. There was a growth of national feeling in some of the nations of Europe, and an increasing desire the ecclesiastical affairs be handled within the nation rather than by the distant papacy, especially as the popes were involved in European politics. There was also a group of men who were fitted for leadership in the establishment of a separate Church. These men were able to accomplish what they did because of the growing consciousness that the Church as then organized and governed was not meeting the needs of the times, nor was it furnishing the moral and spiritual leadership. The Reformation in Germany began through the work of Martin Luther . . . he desired to make sure of his own salvation. **He became an Augustinian monk** and practiced all the austerities of the order but did not

Day Six

find assurance of salvation . . . by his study of the German *mystics,* and especially through the study of the New Testament he came to the belief that a man is not justified by works but by faith alone in Jesus Christ.

This article we have been reading indicates that salvation by belief is not taught in the Catholic Church. The doctrine taught by the Catholic Church is: we are saved by being faithful to the Church and by ceremonies, and then through the process of Purgatory we enter Heaven. There does not seem to be any forgiving of sin except the indulgence from purgatory, given by the pope.

Before Martin Luther's struggle to free Germany from the heavy hand of the pope, a man from Switzerland was trying to reform the Catholic Church in the same manner. The encyclopedia gives this account of him.

The emphases and abridgment by J.A.

John Calvin Swiss reformer of the 16th century.

It was his father's original intention to fit him for the priesthood. . . . he was trained in logic. . . . Up to this point it is safe to presume that his interests and ambitions were purely those of a humanist, and whatever thought he may have had in regard to the need of reform in the matters of Church doctrine and discipline, he doubtless felt with Erasmus and Reuchlin that all reforms that might be required would come about as the result of more complete knowledge.

It was not long after this that he experienced what he calls his "sudden conversion." He writes: "After my heart had long been prepared by the most earnest self-examination, on a sudden the full knowledge of the truth, like a bright light, disclosed to me the abyss of errors in which I was weltering, the sin and shame with which I was defiled." His experience is near of kin to that of Luther's. Yet with all the profound disclosure thus made to him, he still felt no special call to the work of preaching the reformed doctrine and sought only for the undisturbed retirement that would permit him further prosecution of his serious studies. His friend Nicholas Cop had been elected to the rectorship of the University of Paris and at his request Calvin prepared for him an inaugural address which was substantially a defense of the reformed doctrine (1533). To the Sorbonnists this was intolerable, and Calvin was obliged to escape. He returned for a while to his native place, resigned the preferment he held in the Roman Catholic Church and for nearly three years led a wandering life. To escape persecution in France, he fled to Basel, where in 1536, at the age 26, he published his "Institutes." This remarkable work was intended to be a vindication of the Protestant doctrine, and its dedication to the reigning king, Frances I, sought to create royal sympathy for the cause and for its persecuted adherents. By his Catholic opponents his work was styled the "Koran of the heretics."

After completing this work he went to Geneva. . . . The *Duke of Savoy*, unable to secure the submission of Geneva, had by the

Day Six

dent to the lawless and vicious classes what it was they had to contend with, and a wide-reaching opposition began immediately to organize itself. . . . The enmity toward him and his administration was still further fomented by the irrational and merciless severity shown in the punishment of small offenses, such as **the beheading** of a child for striking its mother, the committal of *heretics to the flames*, the eliciting of **testimony by torture**. His rule was one of terror and he was both feared and hated. . . . Dogs in the street were named after him. To antagonize Calvin was a crime, as Castellio found to his coast, and to speak disrespectfully of predestination, as did Bolsec, a felony. But cases like these two are quite eclipsed by the instance of Servetus.

Servetus was a Spaniard, a scholar of independent thought, who convinced himself of the groundlessness of papal claims, but without cordially accepting the theology of Protestantism. In 1531 he published a book entitled (The Errors of the Trinity). Irritated by Calvin's treatment of him and his speculations he retorted upon him and the reformed doctrine flatly and acrimoniously.

Though out of sympathy with the Roman Catholic Church Servetus continued for 20 years in outward conformity with its doctrine and discipline and then wrote another volume under the title (The Restoration of Christianity). This was issued by him during his residence at Vienne and resulted in his arrest at the instance of the archbishop. A copy of the work came under Calvin's eye,

The Cross and The Inquisition

who declared that if Servetus were to come to Geneva he would not get away alive if his authority was sufficient to prevent it. Having escaped from Vienne Servetus did come to Geneva, where his presence soon reached the knowledge of Calvin, who ordered his arrest. Thirty-eight heretical propositions were alleged against him, among others the rejection of the Trinity and speculation leaning toward pantheism: and, although he conducted his defense with vigor and with a degree of acuteness, he was condemned and to the disgrace of the Protestant cause, **was burned** a little way out from Geneva.

The question is: What did the Protestants believe in? What were the Protestants protesting? Didn't they like the teaching and doctrine of the Catholic Church, or was it the awful deeds and crimes of the popes they were protesting? Luther remained a Catholic priest. His quarrel was with the pope. Calvin was not breaking away from the Catholic Church. He only wanted to reform it.

The various Protestant churches that developed after the Reformation *were only man-made religions based on the Catholic Church.* It would be of no value to examine each Protestant Church to find fault with its doctrine. The difference between most of them is found in the communion, that is, understanding the use of the bread and wine. **Originally with the Apostles,** it was one loaf of bread indicating one body — the body of Jesus. Each participant broke off a piece of bread from the same one loaf. They drank from one cup of wine. Now there is no loaf of bread, but individually stamped, pieces of bread and an "individual" glass of grape juice. Some denominations claim it represents the body and blood of Jesus and others say it is only in remembrance of His sacrifice.

Day Six

EASTER

The man-made religions of today still retain many pagan beliefs of the Catholic Church. They are Sun worshippers. On Easter Sunday, they climb up a mountain, before sunrise, and as soon as they see the sun, homing pigeons are released to circle overhead while they worship the goddess of spring. This festival is always held on the day of the week named after the sun — Sunday. The history of Easter is described in the Encyclopedia.

Emphasis by J.A.

Easter is a convergence of three traditions. (1) **Pagan.** According to the Venerable Bede, English historian of the early 8th century, the word is derived from the Norse Ostara or Eostre, meaning the festival of spring at the *vernal equinox,* March 21, when nature is in resurrection after winter. Hence, the rabbits, notable for their fecundity, and the eggs, colored like rays of the returning sun and the northern lights or aurora borealis. The Greek myth, Demeter and Persephone, with its Latin counterpart, Ceres and Persephone, conveys the idea of a goddess returning seasonally from the nether regions to the light of day. (2) Hebrew. In Exodus XII we read of the night in Egypt when the angel of death "passed over" the dwellings of the Israelites, so sparing their first-born. Hence, the Passover or Jewish Pesach, celebrated during Nisan, the first month of the Hebrew year. (3) Christian. It was at the feast of the Passover in Jerusalem that Jesus, a Jew, was crucified and rose from the dead. A

The Cross and The Inquisition

name for Easter, therefor, Pasch, in various spellings, and churches throughout the East and West celebrate Easter as a major feast ranking with **Christmas,** witness the "hot *cross* bun" or boon distributed among the faithful. . . . The Hebrew Passover falls on any day of the week and this did not suit the Christians (Catholics). They wanted a Holy Week beginning with Palm Sunday, proceeding to Good Friday and ending on Easter Sunday, commemorating the resurrection. . . .

— P. W. Wilson

CHRISTMAS

There are Christians who never go to a church, except on Easter and Christmas, two of the most pagan holidays. These two Christian "holy" days are usually occasions when members show off their fine clothes on Easter and get drunk on Christmas.

We should know more about Christmas. The word *Christmas* is really Christ **Mass**. In the Catholic Church, Mass is also called the Eucharist. The priest gives a pantomime act of crucifying Jesus. Than the priest places a thin wafer on the parishioner tongue (that has a *picture of the sun and a cross*). This round wafer, symbolizing Constantine's "Sun and Cross," is supposed to be the broken loaf of bread. Then the priest *drinks the wine.* Lucifer, could not mix it up any better!

We should know more about the festival of Christmas. It is somebody's birthday. I wonder who. The Catholic Church tells us that it is Jesus' birthday. That can't be. Jesus was not born in the middle of winter. Christmas is someone else's birthday — but not that of Jesus.

Do you remember about Lucifer being created? The

Day Six

world was in total darkness at the beginning of the First Day. Then God said, "Let there be light." At that time Lucifer was born. Then there was light for the other half of the First Day. "The evening and the *morning* were the first day."

Celebrating Christmas is a Catholic ritual, invented by the Catholic Pagan Church. There is an account of the beginning of the celebration of Christmas in the *Encyclopedia*. Though the information suggests that all churches were involved and not just the Catholic Church.

> CHRISTMAS, derived from the medieval "Christes Masse," the Mass of Christ; the feast commemorating the birth of Jesus, observed by Christian Churches annually on the 25th of December. It was according to many authorities, **not celebrated** in the first centuries of the Church, as the Christian usage in general was to celebrate *the death* of remarkable persons rather than their birth. The death of the martyr Stephen, and the massacre of the innocents at Bethlehem, had been already long celebrated, when, perhaps in *opposition to the doctrine* of the Manichaeanns respective the "birth" of the Savior, a feast was established in memory of this event in the *4th* century. In the 5th century the Western Church ordered it to be celebrated forever on the day of the **old Roman feast of *the birth of Sol*,** as no certain knowledge of the day of Christ's birth existed. Among the German and Celtic tribes the *winter solstice* was considered an important point of the year, and they held their festival of Yule to commemorate [celebrate] the return of the burning wheel [the sun].

The Cross and The Inquisition

> The holly, the mistletoe, the Yule log, and the wassail bowl are *relics of pre-Christian times*. . . . The custom of making presents at Christmas is derived from ancient usage; but it has become consecrated by ages, ... The Christmas tree has been traced back to the Romans.

The term Christian Church is used throughout this article, which could include all Protestant denominations, but really it is speaking only of the Catholic Church. **The Catholics inaugurated "Christmas."** The ritual of continually crucifying Jesus is called "Mass." The "winter solstice" is the time of year when the night and day are equal. Christmas is Lucifer's birthday.

In the passing of time, many rituals and fables have been added to Christmas, such as Santa Claus and St. Nick. The dictionary gives this meaning to the word *Nick*.

> Nick a masculine name: see Nicholas. n. the Devil; Satan; usually Old Nick.

The name Santa Claus, is explained in the *Encyclopedia*, but the legend about Santa Claus is nothing but a Catholic fable, too ridiculous to copy.

The reformation of the pope's conduct, by Martin Luther in Germany, and by Calvin in Switzerland, caused a loss of prestige. A falling away from the Catholic Church resulted. Finally, to put the Protestant movement in check, the office of Holy Orders declared that all who did not believe as the Catholics were heretics. Those convicted *were tied to a stake and burned to death and all their property was taken over* **by the Church.**

This account is taken from the *Encyclopedia*:

Day Six

Inquisition

Pope Innocent III, in 1199, formally condemned heresy as the most unpardonable of treasons, "Since it is far more grievous to sin against the eternal than against an earthly Majesty." This memorable decree laid the foundation of the Inquisition as an institution **unprecedented in world history**. It was upon this basis that St. Thomas Aquinas bent his genius to build the theory which his faithful followers have held down to the present day. "If false coiners or other felons are justly committed to death without delay by worldly princes, much more may heretics, from the moment that they are convicted, be not only excommunicated, but slain justly out of hand."

The Roman Church, Ecclesia Romana as it was commonly called in the Middle Ages, claimed then, and has never since renounced, the philosophical title of Societas Perfecta: a state in its own right, with powers of legislation over all its subjects and the sanction of punishment over the disobedient, even to the extreme penalty of death. It claims that its subjects are all men or woman who have received Christian baptism, whether deliberately or as *infants at a font*.

The early Christians had differed much from each other; nearly a hundred sects developed in the first hundred years.

If everyone that was baptized deliberately (Protestants) as by the *font*, belonged to the Catholic Church then everyone was a Catholic. They were all subject to

The Cross and The Inquisition

the court of the Catholic Church.

The first hundred years after Jesus all the nations were pagans except the Jews. So, what this article refers to as Christians are really the Roman Pagan Catholics that have adopted and believe in the various pagan versions of the Gospels about Jesus.

The Inquisition lasted for many years, until it was no longer profitable for the Catholic Church.

The inquisition in Spain and Portugal had a peculiar ritual they called *auto-da-fe'*. This is taken from the Encyclopedia.

Emphasis by J.A.

AUTO-DA-FE´, (Portuguese, act of faith), the solemn public act that from 1481 to 1810 [3 hundred years +] was performed in Spain and Portugal at the execution of those condemned to death by the Inquisition. It took the form of a procession through the chief streets of the city or town to the church where a sermon was preached on the true faith, after which, the condemned were turned over to the secular power. The procession was usually witnessed by multitudes, many believing that it was an act of merit to assist at such a function, others **in fear of the terrible Inquisition** lent their presence as a matter of expediency. The procession was led by the *Dominicans*, who were long among the chief inquisitors; they were followed by those who were condemned only to perform public penance. **A great cross** separated these from those condemned to death. The latter were clad in a garment called the san benito, a kind of shirt inscribed with the crimes of the victim and painted with infer-

Day Six

nal symbols. They wore also a pointed cap on the head. Next came effigies of the fugitives and the bones of dead culprits. The rear was brought up by numerous **priests and monks. The most elaborate Auto-da-fe´ was that of Madrid in 1680 under Charles II. The system persisted down to the end of the first decade of the 19th century and five years longer in America, the last recorded event of this kind taking place in Mexico as late as 1815.**

The Catholic Church that established and enforced the Inquisition was certainly not the Church that Jesus built up on the Rock. For Jesus said, "I have come to save not to destroy." It is the Church that Constantine established — "by the cross you shall conquer." The policy of the Catholic Church is to kill all opposition. The office of the *Holy Order* is still in force in the Vatican ready to begin another Inquisition.

Chapter 19

Making the Final Decision

We have gathered a large amount of information about the history of mankind, and man-made religion. Also, we learned much about evolution, from good authority. Still we have not found, *for dead sure*, how the world and all living things came into existence. We are not convinced. We are still in doubt.

Did we hit the jackpot of one chance in a billion that the Earth generated life by accident? Or did a Supreme Being (a Spirit — called God) come into existence by some unknown force and create everything? There still remains a doubt. We will never know for sure who did it. No matter what side we take it will always be based on belief, that is established on believable evidence.

Don't give up. Here is another angle we can work on to support our final decision. Let's see how the creation, during the first "Six Day's," works out.

Are the scientists right when they say that the story of creation does not agree with the laws of nature? Were all things created in their correct and proper order? Was anything neglected that should have been done? Let's go back, to the book of Genesis and read about the creation of the Earth and all the things on it, to find out.

THE FIRST DAY

In the beginning God created the heavens

Day Six

plants yielding seed after their kind, and trees bearing fruit, with seed in them, after their kind; and God saw that it was good. And there was evening and there was morning, a third day.

We will have to consider many of today's known scientific facts to really understand all that took place during this third day. The first commandment from God was for the water to be gathered into one place. That is, the water that is left after a great quantity of the water was drawn away from the earth into outer space.

The water, that was left on the Earth, was drawn into one place by the creation of gravity. We know what gravity is able to do, it draws everything towards the center of the earth — even air is pulled toward the center of the earth. Today we have magnets that attract iron, but have no influence on other substance such as air. Gravity is something man would like to understand, and be able to control. The strong pull of gravity shrunk the earth into a condensed tight ball, and In so doing, the thin crust of the earth wrinkled into some very high mountains and deep canyons

Then God commanded the dry land to appear. In a *National Geographic* is an artist's drawing of the continents being exuded from the earth. The land, *that was composed of granite (not igneous rock)*, lifted straight up (from the igneous rock) so that it extended above sea level. Last of all, God commanded that vegetation, of all kinds, should grow. Many species are now extinct.

It's strange that vegetation would be created before the sun. Vegetation needs light in order to grow. In the Bible we are told that God is light. Lucifer, the bearer of light, was created during the first day. By Lucifer, light was continuously carried from God to the earth. This light was *constant*, not like the light from the sun twelve hours on and twelve hours off.

The fossils that have been found, indicate that the growth of all kinds of vegetation was terrific. Some had huge trunks, and were over one hundred feet tall.

No animals or bugs were here, at this time, to destroy the vegetation. Things grew to their maturity and new growth kept coming up, building many layers of ferns, leaves and trunks of the old vegetation This debris eventually turned to coal. The Third Day also lasted seven thousand years.

FOURTH DAY

> Then God said, "Let there be lights in the expanse of the heavens to separate the day from the night, and let them be for signs, and for seasons, and for *days and years*; and let them be for lights in the expanse of the heavens to give light on the earth"; and it was so. And God made the two great lights, the greater light to govern the day, and the lesser light to govern the night; He made the stars also. And God placed them in the expanse of the heavens to give light on the earth, and to govern the day and the night, and to separate the light from the darkness; and God saw that it was good. And there was evening and there was morning, a fourth day.

Now that the sun and the moon are created, God no longer gives light to the earth. God must have had a reason for changing the good and perfect light to that of the sun. Now the sunlight only shines for twelve hours, and then everything is in darkness for the same length of time.

Day Six

Why did God make this change in the illuminating system? Lucifer, the medium on which light travels, committed a grievous sin by becoming proud and thinking of making herself equal with God. God is now establishing a system whereby he can destroy Lucifer. This account is given in the Bible through the prophet Ezekiel, who is called the son of man. Lucifer is spoken of as King of Tyre. As we read, explanations will be inserted.

> "Son of man, take up a *lamentation* over the *king* of Tyre, and say to him, Thus says the Lord God, 'You had the seal of perfection, full of wisdom and perfect in beauty. You were in Eden, the garden of God; . . . ."

(Lucifer was in the garden of God when she tempted Eve.)

> "You were the anointed cherub who covers, ..."

(No human being was ever called a cherub.)

> "and I placed you there. You were on the holy mountain of God; you walked in the midst of the stones of fire."

(The stones of fire are the stars that God created at this time.)

> "You were blameless in your ways from the day you were created, until unrighteousness was found in you. By the abundance of your trade you were internally filled with violence, and you sinned; therefore I have cast you as profane from the mountain of God. *And I have destroyed* you, O covering cherub,

And I have destroyed you, O covering cherub, from the midst of the stones of fire. Your heart was lifted up because of your beauty; you corrupted your wisdom by reason of your splendor. I cast you to the ground; I put you before kings, that they may see you. By the multitude of your iniquities, in the unrighteousness of your trade, you profaned your sanctuaries. Therefore I have brought fire from the *midst of you*; it has consumed you, and I have turned you to ashes on the earth in the eyes of all who see you. All who know you among the peoples are appalled at you; you have become terrified, and you will be no more.'"

Ezekiel 28: 12-20

God says, "I have brought fire from the midst of you. That indicates the stars are within Lucifer which will burn her to ashes. God speaks of Lucifer's destruction as if it had already happened. The reason God speaks this way is, when God determines to do something it is so sure to happen that He speaks as if it already took place.

Contrary to the scientists' belief, the Earth was formed first and then the Sun. We know that the moon has a gravity influence on the Earth because it causes tides. The moon revolving around the Earth acts like a dynamo causing the earth to develop internal heat to the extent of developing volcanoes all over the world that erupt and spew out hot lava.

There are many such planets with moons revolving around them. Some planets have several moons that make them very hot — all are sending out a strong magnetic current of gravity.

The Universe is set up in such a manner that every-

Day Six

thing is revolving on its axis, and also revolving around the sun. This tremendous force that the planets are sending out is causing the sun to get so hot that it becomes a hot ball of vapor — over ten million degrees.

The sun is not consuming some of its material to stay white hot nor are there atomic explosions to cause this heat. The sun remains a hot vapor by the planets revolving around it. The other suns that we call stars, also have planets revolving around them so that they too stay perpetually hot and bright.

FIFTH DAY

Then God said, "Let the waters teem with swarms of living creatures, and let birds fly above the earth in the open expanse of heaven." And God created the great sea monsters, and every living creature that moves, with which the waters swarm after their kind, and every winged bird after its kind; and God saw that it was good. And God blessed them, saying, "Be fruitful and multiply, and fill the waters in the seas, and let birds multiply on the earth." And there was evening and there was mourning, a fifth day.

The scientists have it figured that the fish were the beginning of all living things. Consider this fact, if so, what did the fish have to eat? If there was no vegetation the floor of the ocean would be bare rock and sand. Also the land would be bare.

Because vegetation was created first, the ocean was full of seaweed, moss and many kinds of plants for the fish to eat. Birds of many kinds and size were created. They also had plenty to eat. The birds had all the fruit

Making the Final Decision

and nuts from the many trees, and seeds from grass and shrubs.

SIXTH DAY

Then God said, "Let the earth bring forth living creatures after their kind: cattle and creeping things and beasts of the earth after their kind"; and it was so.

And God *made* the beasts of the earth after their kind, and the cattle after their kind, and every thing that creeps on the ground after its kind; and God saw that it was good.

Then God said, "Let us make man in Our image, according to Our likeness; and let them rule over the fish of the sea and over the birds of the sky and over the cattle and over all the earth, and over every creeping thing that creeps on the earth."

And God created man in His own image, in the image of God He created him; male and female He created them. . . .

And there was evening and there was morning, the sixth day.

The Bible gives this account about everything that was created in the order they were created. Nothing is wrong in the order that was given. Everything is positive, showing no doubt or the possibility that it may have happened some other way. Still it is something the individual has to believe.

By the account given in the Bible, man was exposed to death because **he didn't believe God about not eating the fruit of good and evil.** Now man is given

Day Six

another chance to *believe*. If we knew for sure about God, then there would be no room for belief.

According to the Hebrew Bible, if we "believe" that God sent his **word** to become the "son of man" and believe in the son's promise of "Eternal Life," death will have no power over us. There is no hope of "Eternal Life" in believing in the various theories of evolution.

Because this decision, that is based on belief, is so crucial we should find more material to base our decision on. Let's study the story about the deluge, and see if such a cataclysm could have happened. Maybe this legend is but a preposterous ancient fable.

According to Hebrew records this devastating flood happened about two thousand years after Adam and Eve. This is a synopsis of the account as written in the Scripture.

THE DELUGE

> Then the Lord saw that the wickedness of man was great.... And the Lord said, "I will blot out man whom I have created from the face of the land I will send rain on the earth forty days and forty nights; and I will blot out from the face of the land every living thing that I have made."... all the fountains of the great deep burst open, and the floodgates of the sky were opened.
>
> Genesis 6:5-7

No matter how hard it rained in those forty days and nights the Earth would not be covered with water. Rainwater comes from the oceans and runs off the land, returning to the ocean. If all the ice in the Arctic and Antarctic were to melt, it would only raise the ocean

Making the Final Decision

waters about two feet. The water that is under ground is negligible to flooding the land. Therefor there must have been other sources of water available in order to cover all the high mountains. Let's read that account again.

> . . . on the same day all the fountains of the great deep burst open, and the **floodgates of the sky were opened.**

Does the sky have floodgates? This statement means something else took place. The sky is the space above us. It extends as high as there is air.

The air was parted, in places, like floodgates and permitted ice, from the extreme cold of outer space, to fall to the Earth. This ice is from the vast amount of water that originally covered the Earth. For forty days this ice poured in through the floodgates. The enormous volume of this extremely cold ice from outer space raised the water level in the oceans to the very top of the tallest mountain. This ice, that was piled miles high, was frozen solid to the very bottom of the ocean. When this ice was forced to float, by the rising water, the ocean floor of rocks was torn loose. As these huge ice bergs moved they scooped out depressions on the face of the Earth, (which later became basins for lakes). When the ice moved to warmer water rocks fell from the bottom. The scientists recognize the scars and rocks left by this vast volume of ice and call it "The Ice Age."

The flood of water covered the Earth completely, and every living thing drowned, thus bringing to an end (exterminating) the dinosaurs. Within forty days there were no living things left on the land.

The continual rain caused mud-slides that washed trees and animals and people into the deep canyons — covering them deep with mud and rocks. These fossil remains we are now uncovering.

Day Six

If you are capable of making a decision, now is the time to choose what you are going to belief. Do not decide in haste. First consider all that we have studied and criticized. When you think you are capable of making an intelligent decision then decide what you are willing to believe. I advise you to be careful that you make the right decision! You will not get a second chance after you are dead!

Order Form

This is a limited edition.

To order additional copies of *Day Six* please send $9.95 for each book by check or money order to:

Joe Allard Enterprises
74490 Laurelwood Road
Rainier, OR 97048

Do not send cash. (Orders must be prepaid.)

The price of books ordered with this form includes the cost of postage and handling plus any applicable sales tax. .

This is a limited edition. Please allow 4-6 weeks for delivery.

Your name: _____

Mailing Address: _____

City: _____

State: _____ Zip _____

Number of books ordered @ $9.95 Total _____

Total payment _____

DATE DUE

NO 23 '92			
DE 30 '92			
NO 18 '93			
DE 19 '94			
DE 4 '95			
AP 30 '97			
DE 10			

```
BT              36202
712
.A44    Allard, Joe
1991        Day six.
```

HIEBERT LIBRARY
Fresno Pacific College - M.B. Seminary
Fresno, CA 93702